The Great THEATRE of the SALE

The Trusted Advisor Selling Approach to Mastering the Heart and Soul of Selling

Brad Tonini

TRUSTED ADVISOR PRESS

1213/1 Queens Road, Melbourne, Australia

brad@bradtonini.com

ISBN: 978-0-6489112-2-7 PAPERBACK

ISBN: 978-0-6489112-0-3 PAPERBACK

ISBN: 978-0-6489112-1-0 HARDBACK

Cover and interior design *LRB Publishing Services*

contact@lindaruthbrooks.com

Nonfiction/sales education/

The Great Theatre of the Sale is a sales instruction manual, designed to assist salespersons of all areas to gain valuable information on ways to optimise sales opportunities through presentation, high standard behaviour and becoming trusted advisors to their clients. Every attempt has been made to give appropriate acknowledgment for material, visual or written.

Dedication

To the Tonini Team at home – my wife Pauline, Joshua and Mac and Matilda.

Thank you for your unconditional love and support and for being my heroes on an exciting journey called life.

Other books by Brad Tonini

Time for Life

Make it Happen Now!

The New Rules of the Game

101 Ways to Keep the Sales Focus

Sales 101

7 Keys to Presenting Ideas That Sell

Contents

INTRODUCTION

The Magic of Selling is its Theatre

Where have all the salespeople gone?

In an age now where likes, connections and friends seem to be the talk of the town, we have lost our way to what is truly important to the success of a salesperson: the metric of a converted sale.

The business fundamental of creating a converted new piece of business—a client—will never lose its importance.

After training and mentoring salespeople for over 20 years, I have noticed we have moved to the side tried and proven techniques and the sharpening of our people skills and replaced these life skills with an ability to post meaningless, self-ingratiating posts about what we had for breakfast.

There are plenty of people advertising and spruiking different ways to "fill up the pipeline" and to create quality leads when a good deal of the time they result in minimal conversion.

How about the marketer who says he can make a fortune from home working in his jammies? Gimme a break!

Call me old fashioned, a dinosaur perhaps, but I judge myself and those I coach on the old fashioned signed order and money in the bank.

My father Neville Tonini was a great salesperson. He was a true entrepreneur who was one of the few pioneers of direct and incentive marketing in Australia. In his early years, the foundational years, he was a retail salesperson for a retail electrical in Centre Rd, Bentleigh in Melbourne Victoria.

His lessons with me across the breakfast table were simple: 'Get face-to-face with your buyer and your chance to convert will automatically go up.' Simple stuff.

He knew how to sell, how to get people engaged. His raw level of passion alone for the solution and his ability to ask a question and simply shut up and listen was first class. He's probably the reason why so many of my clients say to me, 'You are a pretty good listener.'

But Dad also knew the value of getting in front of the buyer, to see the whites of their eyes.

He always said it was harder for someone to knock you back when you are in front of them, and you could also deal with any uncertainties if you could sense them!

I ask the question now in my workshops, 'How many of you believe you'll increase your conversion rate when you get face-to-face?' Every hand in the room goes up. They agree that they will convert more sales if they get in the presence of their client.

Why don't they do it more often?

They get caught up in busy work, sending out emails, and trying to be "productive" by getting quotes out and off their desk.

I often say in the classroom we are not in the **proposals** business, we are in the **results** business.

And… this is where theatre comes into it. Our ability to convert business by using creativity to create influence in the sales process. Theatre turns the unreal into something real.

Selling is the same. Selling is a people sport. We warm to the human touch. You cannot conjure magic from afar. You can't do it online. You can only conjure up the magic of the moment if you're there.

We talk about the commoditisation trap today—the difficulty in creating a position that is truly yours. The internet has created that, making everyone seemingly an expert and authority.

This is where theatre comes into its own to make you memorable; it is a form of differentiation, and the richer the experience, the more theatre.

There's an old saying in sales: “People buy on emotion and justify with logic.” Email has no emotion. In other words, facts, numbers, and all the sensible stuff makes the purchase seem logical. But the want rather than the need is what makes the deal.

If you can’t connect, there is no theatre. And if you take the theatre out of selling, impersonal selling is all that remains.

A hundred years ago (or so), people in remote areas bought everything through mail order catalogues. The online equivalent is what’s happening now. We’re going backwards. Unless you get face-to-face, you cannot breathe life into your product.

The other way to buy was when the travelling salesman came to town with his pots and pans or other products and he would set himself up in the town and then go door to door to sell his wares.

That's selling… real selling.

Totally commission based, staying away from home in long periods, and not eating unless you have sold something.

Ever seen that movie about McDonald's with Michael Keaton playing Ray Kroc? It was a clever movie about a salesman and his desire to take control of the McDonald's hamburger business and franchise it across the world.

It was interesting to watch Ray's humble beginnings travelling across the USA selling milkshake makers and making a living.

He was that travelling salesman I just talked about, the one who went from town to town showing the milkshake maker and then ringing back to the office from the phone booth in the next town to see if they had received a faxed order from the café or diner.

I guess I am talking about the real art and theatre of selling. The art of influence and persuasion, but persuasion for good! That's exactly what has been lost: the adrenalin rush from a sales call with someone whom you need to create a persuasive win–win argument to buy something.

I believe that selling is a noble profession , in fact I would argue that not only does "nothing happen in business until the sale is made" (not mine, an old expression), but that it's up to each and every one of us in the business context and perhaps even in life to understand that we are all selling something.

Selling in its raw essence is about presenting a persuasive and compelling business case that is in the other person's self-interest to create action.

That self-interest could be to make more money, to reduce the risk in their business, to take the hassle out of business, or perhaps even to get a market share advantage on a competitor. But then, selling is also the personal sale we make as well to everyone we come in contact with.

I think Daniel Pink said it well when he called his book *To Sell is Human*. So correct.

Each day in life we apply for a new job, go to the interview, ask your boss for a promotion. You are selling! Not only selling, but you are also using theatre and you may not even know it.

If you have young kids, you will know what I mean. They sell from a young age. If they want to do something or to get something (like ice cream), they soon learn how to get enthusiastic cooperation.

So what happens to us and why do some adults look down on the profession?

Well, the answer lies in those before us who ripped people off, who wanted to make money, or who just were plain greedy. They were salespeople who preyed upon naïve buyers, whether it be at the home or at the office. There have been plenty of movies made about over the years. Just look up *Tin Men* or *The Wolf of Wall Street* and you get the picture. This is the stuff that makes the profession lack integrity, long term credibility and is at odds with the trusted advisor approach.

I feel like I need to define a little about what I mean when I say theatre in this book.

This book is written in a business context and with the professional or novice salesperson in mind. The person who each day is charged with the responsibility of making something happen. To create the visible out of the invisible.

Theatre in the sales context is all about influence, persuasion, script writing, stage setting, directing, and character creation. Without a plan, without some understanding of the play you are in, you are merely turning up and there is no guarantee of success (Woody Allen may have thought differently).

So if this is a play and we are actors, is it for real? Good question. Yes, this is the point of distinction I want to make. Theatre in the selling sense needs to be very real to be able to enjoy longevity in the profession. It's all about careful attention to trust and doing what you say you will. But… it's also about making sure there is integrity and an offering of products and services that actually help the buyer in their business.

Research conducted by the Salesforce Group claims that only 24 percent of all salespeople spend face-to-face time with buyers. No wonder I'm appalled!

Face-to-face time guides customers to the important "moment of truth" and you can't get that without the art of persuasion. But that's the life of a busy salesperson—meetings, quoting, product knowledge, chasing up orders to make sure there are no issues—and sometimes the job that they are actually getting paid to do takes the "leftover" time.

So how come the new salesperson doesn't place as high a level of importance on the meeting in front of a buyer as much as other tasks? Why the move away from crafting your sales presentation and putting as much time into your face-to-face time as you do to your Facebook likes?

I think we find ourselves in an interesting place. A place where we want the results, but I am not so sure that we are prepared to do the work. So perhaps this theatre stuff requires us to be a contrarian, someone who is prepared to push against the current, to do what others are simply not doing.

To be that contrarian sales professional, we need to understand that great theatre is like guerrilla intelligence: it gives a competitive edge in selling.

I am not talking about being someone you aren't, to put on show for the sake of it. I am talking about being congruent to who you are but to also be buyer aware and centric.

Universities spit out marketing graduates with next to no sales experience. In fact, when I did my degree, it had one sales subject in the whole degree program: sales presentation and negotiation. It's almost like selling doesn't have its own identity in tertiary education.

So what are we going to have to push up against to put this whole idea of theatre up the priority order in sales?

Well, I think it starts with us re-thinking some of the societal norms that we are seeing in society.

Firstly, I am not sure we want to engage with each other.

Have you stepped into an elevator recently and then watched as everyone looks down at their phone and scrolls through social media or text messages that are meaningless? What's wrong with us? To even get a "good morning" is a big deal.

Selling is like that. Asking someone to return your call to

have a conversation with you is more challenging. But show me a salesperson who places a high value on it and gets results by really understanding their buyer and I will pay more for that.

The second thing I think that is taking place is **we are becoming less confrontational** in business.

It's so easy to say no by email and it's so easy for a salesperson to give up. So we all email the buyer and then hope they will buy or we invite them into a group and start this subtle but not-so-subtle influencing style stuff.

The third reason why we have moved away from the theatre of selling is **that it takes time and requires work and thinking to make it work.**

We are impatient today and want instant gratification, which means that making those nurturing calls or repeated sales calls to advance the sale is not taking place.

This book is all about the real selling—to sell when you don't look like you are selling and to be a true trusted advisor and not an order taker by mastering the theatre of the sale.

Enjoy the journey as we explore some parallels with theatre and also the age-old methods of theatre that get results in sales.

Part A

The Whole World is a Sales Stage

Be the Director of Your Own Sales Call

When placed in charge, take charge. Choreograph your sales call so that it gradually moves towards the desired end result. It doesn't have to be dramatic. In fact, it's best if it's not.

It's show time, it's time to shine and make an impression.

Every minute of the dance we perform with the buyer has its own context and fabric, but one of the most underrated skills we can have as an experienced salesperson is to carefully choreograph and direct the sale. Our job as a professional salesperson is to always have planned spontaneity.

The Trusted Advisor Approach to Selling

As we discuss the "director role" we play in a sales conversation, I think it's important to define the premise and assumption that runs through this book. I am firm believer that great career salespeople need to see themselves as trusted advisors to their clients and prospects.

The trusted advisor is the "go–to" person in their industry that all other salespeople would love to become. The authority, thought leader, and that person who holds enormous magnetism to buyers. They are the high performers over the long term and develop a loyal, repeatable, and referrable client base who just keep buying. They are also the ones who understand the need for the great theatre of the sale as a key part of their arsenal in converting sales. So the trusted advisor believes that by being the director of the sales call, they are in control of the sales process and can therefore influence the result.

You wouldn't expect the actor to turn up and just improvise the whole show, nor the director to say to the cast "just make it up as you go along." The same applies to salespeople; a well-crafted presentation that engages has to be planned.

As I said, the theatre of the sale depends not only on what you give but also what you "give off," so give off sign-vehicles that direct the conversation where you want it to go. Use small cues, like picking up the catalogue, presenting with relevant items, and make comments that naturally segues towards your end.

Take some time and work out how this appointment will go; have a plan B should it not go to plan.

Maintaining expressive control requires making sure that as many events as possible work in your favour. To achieve this, you need to keep the steering wheel in your hand. You're the director, remember? Don't allow little things to distract.

Okay, the situation has shifted from the meet-and-greet, the preamble, and the settling in. What is now required is a display of your professional competence. So, ask yourself: how do I want my buyer to respond as a result of my call? Another meeting? More information? Meeting their superior? Or a full close? Work all aspects of your performance to this end.

The Rhythm of the Sale

Every sales call has a rhythm, and that rhythm goes through cycles. Buyers get engaged and then they don't. They get re-engaged again, then they lose a bit of interest. In a 10, 20, 30, or 60-minute sales call, you have many opportunities to change that rhythm (if you choose to) by creating impression management waves.

Most salespeople I work with don't understand this. They think a sales call is "just a sales call," but it's more than that. Each sales call is a "customer experience," an experience where we create an environment that resembles a stage production.

You've already defined the situation, created a set, directed the action, and presented yourself. You are now guiding the beat of the conversation while looking out for opportunities. "Is it a conversion opportunity or a positioning opportunity?" is a good question to ask yourself.

In other words, "Can I convert this opportunity today or is it about positioning our business for future opportunities?" The answer indicates your role, because if you push too hard, you may be over-emphasing your part.

The internet commoditisation of selling has made the face-to-face sales call gold in its weight and impact. Underplay it—treat it much less—and you do so at your own peril. You may not get another chance in the short term. It needs rehearsal, a screen play and script written with real features and benefits, role playing, and scenario scoping based on buyer response.

Show time is theatre time and everything matters.

What small scenes are you playing out in front of your buyer?

How will you choreograph them for real impact?

What discussion points need to be covered?

How will you get their attention and are there subplots to be played out?

All thought for the director.

It's Not a Sales Call, It's a Customer Experience

I think where we miss the point in sales is that we undervalue the buyer's time. This is why the buyer doesn't always like to give us the time to come and show us our solution; they are worried that if they get into a conversation with us, it is going to use up valuable time,

They want to preserve their time as they always have things they are juggling and they have a perception that most things really don't have much point of difference anyway, so why waste time?

The onus is on us to not only be prepared but also to carefully consider how we are going to make a real impact. How we are going to treat this golden time truly as a moment of truth where we may not get that opportunity again.

Each customer sales experience has a beginning, middle, and end. The key is to lay out a foundation to an ideal meeting and how you can create a wonderful context as well as your content.

Choreographing the Customer Experience

If we are entertaining and educating the buyer, don't we need to really think about the journey we want to take the buyer on? Here are some thought-starters to consider when thinking about crafting this experience to make it truly memorable for the buyer. Being the director of your own sales call means focusing on:

1. Staging an experience: what will they remember about you?
2. How you will make your entry into the meeting?
3. How will you get into your true character?
4. Knowing how you want the buyer to feel and act after you have gone
5. Understanding your personal brand: dressing, grooming
6. Timing and pacing of the meeting
7. Emotional performance and passion for what you do
8. Creating selling vignettes, little opportunities to transfer knowledge about your solution and how it will help them
9. Revealing your solution with great sense of anticipation
10. Creation of drama
11. Creating a script of what needs to be covered, questions to be asked
12. How you will gesture or move your body

In Part B of this book, you will find specific techniques that are aimed to make these elements of the performance stand out by getting into character.

If you've laid the appropriate groundwork, it increases the chances of the performance working in your favour. Make it interesting. Make it exciting. What follows are some components of your performance for which you have set the stage and are appropriately costumed.

Putting on the Mask and Getting into Character

English playwright William Shakespeare said, "All the world is a stage…" Someone else added, "…but we don't know which bits." Selling is like that. You're saying hello one minute and you're on stage the next.

You are required to play innumerable roles. We all have to. Lots of different people inhabit your body. Let's talk about back-stage and front-stage behaviour.

Back-stage is where you play a role other than your professional selling role.

It's the not-for-the-customer role. Playing backyard cricket with your kids, that's back-stage. Politics, religion, hobbies, sex, etc., is all back-stage stuff.

When someone knocks on your door, you've got to quickly decide which of your several selves will answer. Should you present as a salesperson? Or will the situation require you to drop that role in favour of one of the many others you also play: parent, son/daughter, sibling, friend, fan, parishioner, constituent, hobbyist, sportsperson, customer and so on.

This book targets your role in sales, which is obviously a cornerstone of your life otherwise you wouldn't be reading this. Customers expect you to play the part of salesperson and to be "in character" If you don't, they label you as being "unprofessional."

When on-stage, you are expected to act according to the conventions of business. But if I were your customer, I would be peering between the cracks, wondering to what extent you are acting when describing your product in such glowing terms. Is it really as good as you're telling me? Do you mean your words? Do you really love your product or are you just saying that because that's what you're paid to say?

Given that you've spent a lot of time with your product, you've probably convinced yourself it's the best on the market. But if you don't believe your own argument, the rest of this book isn't going to ride easy, especially not my thoughts around trusted advisor selling. So learn to love your product.

Social media and the current emailable sales environment has made selling very impersonal compared to how it used to be.

Unfortunately, it costs nothing to post something, so we now get bombarded by people who would not normally be in selling playing the numbers game. They send out thousands of emails to people they don't know and they hope like crazy they can hook a buyer. That's not selling.

There is no theatre in social media. An email has no personality. But YOU do, when you knock on their door and grab their attention. If you can put them at ease right away, you've reached first base.

The credibility of the moment requires that the buyer must be drawn in. To be truly convincing, you must live the role you are presently performing.

The buyer is playing a role too. If s/he has agreed to the meeting, the buyer *wants* to be drawn in.

Think for a minute: at the end of the meeting with a salesperson, have you, as a buyer, ever found yourself feeling disappointed that the salesperson didn't pay enough attention to you or that s/he didn't ask questions that showed some homework had been done? Or perhaps s/he just didn't look engaged and take an active, sincere interest in you?

Putting on a mask means a number of things in selling.

It starts with the idea that we are "always on show" in selling, understanding that the customer is always the customer and buyer.

The mask is always on to let the customer know that we are positive, to create a perception in the mind of the buyer that things will always be okay.

The mask allows us to be confident, powerful, or charismatic. It gives us an opportunity to play a part which will increase our magnetism.

The character is now being formed.

To be effective as a character in sales, we need to be believable, real, trustworthy, someone who people can relate to. It's this character who claims the loyalty of the customer.

A properly formed character in sales is someone who translates the script into a piece of theatre, by using non-verbals, facial expressions, tonality, pace, and knows when there needs to be emphasis on a structure or impromptu response.

In *The Presentation of Self in Everyday Life* by Erving Goffmann, he talks about "impression management" and says to "assume that when an individual appears before others he will have many motives for trying to control the impression they receive of the situation. There is a popular view that the individual offers his performance and puts on a show for the benefit of other people."

I think this is what we do in sales; we make an impression. It is for the benefit of our customer and to improve their position.

Back-Stage and Front-Stage

Ensure your back-stage is more or less consistent with your front-stage. When a prospect catches you playing a role that is way out of character for your professional self, that prospect will have glimpsed an aspect of your back-stage you may not have wanted to reveal. That makes for an awkward moment, but they'll overlook it unless it creates a genuine conflict of credibility. You see, it's okay to *stretch* your character, but it's not okay to *fall out* of character.

Customers accept small inconsistencies when the working day is through, but they can't accept contradictions. Nor should they.

An example of a contradiction is playing the same role for a rival product. Which is best? You can't say both. Here's another example of getting roles mixed up: working for a financial regulator by day and a financial institution by night. My tip: keep your back-stage pristine. (Several politicians should have taken that advice.)

Another example of when I have found this in conflict in my sales career was when a client has asked me to enjoy a social occasion with them and their partner or has invited me to their Christmas party or corporate box at the football stadium.

I guess I have always been guarded about showing too much of myself and that includes letting the guard down with alcohol. I get invited a lot to the dinner before or after a sales conferences as a professional speaker and consultant and this can be even more challenging.

As their trusted advisor to the sales team, you know that they see you in a certain light. Remember, you will be back there, say, three weeks from now teaching them another aspect of selling!

I create congruence in my appearance, my look, and my actions. I believe as the trusted advisor sales professional, walking your talk is mission critical.

The other distinction I make is that it's not okay to not walk your talk when you are giving professional advice.

I have a real challenge with listening to the financial planner or investment expert who doesn't have any investments and then jumps into his old beaten up Holden when he is giving you advice as to how to invest $250k.

Similarly, the business coach who has never owned a business with "real employees" and a responsibility to an overdraft or some debt in their business who spruiks how you can make "money in your jammies" and that is all very easy.

Back to the face-to-face sales call...

The situation you are about to enter will require definition—that is the reason for your call. The better you formalise the purpose of the meeting, the easier will be everything that follows, and that defines everybody's role, theirs as well as yours. Having agreed that you are playing the part of salesperson implies that their role is "potential buyer."

"Who invited who?" is another question that helps clarify the situation. If they have invited you, the energy is stronger. Are they a referred opportunity? Again, this helps define the situation. If they want to talk to you, they are a warm prospect. This allows you to assume territory you would otherwise play hard to win. Questions like this define the situation and allow you to weigh up your sales strategy in advance.

Sometimes the situation is not defined at all. You have to bend general circumstances into a sales situation. This can be a big ask, changing a situation from whatever it is into one that's about you and your solution.

Better: sort out the reason for meeting beforehand. Otherwise, it is almost a cold call.

Hopefully you've won agreement about the reason for your call, if not you'll be manoeuvring the conversation as cleverly as you can, while trying not to come across "like a salesperson."

Building Your Stage Set and Your Use of Props

The stage we set is everything. It allows us to move comfortably inside and for us to express our intent. It allows us to assume some control and to set up a successful result. We know inside that stage where we are strong and commanding, where we are most vulnerable.

The trusted advisor salesperson spends time on their stage set and acquaints themselves with any space that is not theirs quickly.

Your Space

When designing your own space, position things so the customer will naturally move into the area where you want them to be. That should be a seat they won't have to shift from when you want to display something because everything you'll want to show should be close to hand.

Once you've got customers settled, you don't want them unsettled.

When your client plans to call on you, check which works best—inside your inner sanctum or in neutral boardroom space?

Inside will reveal a lot about you.

If your office is a mess, too downmarket, or unsuitable in other ways, whisk the client away elsewhere. Conversely, if your office builds credibility and puts the necessary information at your fingertips, invite them in.

You hold the control button when you're on your own turf. Design your set to handle every type of performance. What do you need? Armchairs? Chairs? Side tables? PowerPoints? Samples? Spreadsheets? Whiteboard? Computer set-ups?

Check the seating. Make it easy for your prospect to settle in the room. Get it all sorted. Offer a coffee when s/he arrives.

I have a client who presents out of hotel suites their new range of men's suits to their buyers. They spend big on the right view from the right hotel room to make an impression with a very fancy coffee machine at the ready.

If you are writing up big orders for big retailers, you need to wow.

When I was in the corporate promotional product business, many of the suppliers would have their showrooms dressed up to kill. Nothing was spared.

Again, the idea was to take the buyer on a journey with you. A number of the Chinese suppliers in Hong Kong I dealt with on a sourcing mission were also masters at this!

Their Space

When you call on a prospect, we know there is a certain advantage of being able to be in neutral space like a boardroom, especially where there are visual aids like whiteboards, etc. to be able to explain your solution or to sell your credibility if you are selling services.

Inside their office is loaded with their stuff. Maybe you want that to better understand the client; pictures, awards, and holiday snaps are all great rapport builders. You can't always control this aspect, but you may be able to angle towards where you feel best suited—or maybe not. Do the best you can in their space and sit where you're told. Take it easy, keep it natural, adapt, entertain, and keep it light.

That being fixed, you will have freed yourself to perform in front of them, around them, or wherever suits. First, you're going to entertain until you've captured interest. Live the role of advisor and impart information beautifully tied to their major payoffs or benefits.

Be as succinct and as interesting as you know how.

As I said, if it's on your turf, you can better direct the set design. When it's not your space, you'll have different and fewer options. However, there are ways to overwhelm a room without it actually being your own.

You can change the setting and control someone else's space simply by showing a short film clip on your laptop or running through some PowerPoint and going to a neutral table.

Everybody will gather around your screen—there's nowhere else to be. And you'll have them all staring at whatever you want them to be looking at.

Never underestimate the power of a great view if you are presenting and hosting from your office. My office is just off St. Kilda Road in Melbourne overlooking Albert Park Lake and I wish I had a dollar for every time a potential customer asked me, 'Wow, do you ever get tired of this view?'

What a great rapport builder, what a great piece of theatre.

Already you have created an impression, a lasting one at that.

The next piece of my theatre of first impression is to offer each person a coffee. Initially, I might get a 'no thanks,' but then when they realise that I was referring to a barista-made cappuccino, or any other variation on that, personally delivered to the suite on a tray in a matter of minutes, they quickly change their mind.

I haven't made my own coffee for years when visitors come by and it's a memorable experience. The bills are as big as a small car payment on a big month, but hey, that's just a cost of doing business.

Preparing Your "Entry"

> ***Great salespeople own their space and set the scene quickly. A firm handshake, a smile, and being "on" are all examples of being present with your buyer.***

Look for a rapport builder, something your read about their industry, something from their website or social media posts. Consider saying something like…

'I couldn't help but notice when I was on your website the other night…'

People love to know you have done some work, done some

research on them and their industry. People don't have time to educate you.

By the way, try that approach in your meeting and watch what happens. They will ask more often than not (about 50 percent of the time), 'How did you find the site?' or, 'We are doing work on the site right now.'

I remember going into a trusted professional's meeting room and they had a whole presentation and solutions all loaded up in the iPad and they proceeded to show me parts of the solution on the big screen as we walked around their showroom.

Not only did that allow them to move around and be present with me while displaying their ideas, but they were also a master at creating great tension when the automated screen came down from the ceiling on cue.

The old expression "you don't get a second chance to make a first impression" is true. When you give some thought as to how you want to appear in the first 30 seconds, things start to happen.

Many years ago, in the 90s, there was a show on television, *Tonight Live with Steve Vizard* (showing my age), and it just so happened that I looked like the host Steve Vizard as many people told me. On one occasion, a great friend of mine, Natalie, got me on the show to do a skit with Steve.

As it turned out, it included Elle Macpherson (will expand in the next book some day) and I still have a signed calendar from Elle to prove the story.

Anyway, I digress.

The point is that the show was very popular. In fact, it rated like crazy and this was a big help to me! I used it all to my advantage. I decided to dress how he would dress and I had the same height and weight on my side, which was a massive advantage. I wish I had a dollar for the number of times I was greeted at reception by the gatekeeper and then the decision maker with the opening comment, 'Has anyone ever told you that you look like Steve Vizard?'

Of course, I played along with it all and appeared like it was the first time anyone had made such a comment. Keeping the joke alive was the next job, to let them keep remembering me.

It started to get more and more popular with all my clients while I was out doing sales calls and allowed me to segue into the fact that I had been on the show and met Steve, etc. What a great ice breaker, an entry that lasted more than two to three minutes at last!

Using Props with Great Effect

Everything matters. Every seemingly small accessory can make an impact and help to tell a congruent story to the buyer.

Let's look at some really important props of the trusted advisor: the car, the dress, and accessories.

The car you arrive in can set the scene.

I am always amazed by the number of salespeople who over the years have told me that one of their strategies was to arrive in an old model car to an appointment. The theory is that the potential client would think the salesperson has too much money and that they would be overcharged.

That doesn't make a whole lot of sense to me as I have always found that a buyer is always more attracted to the advice I can give when I have a luxury car all cleaned and gleaming at them.

The only time I would see an exception to the rule was when I was doing consulting work in agricultural sales and calling on farmers. It would have been inappropriate to not be in the company branded Hi-ace, but that doesn't mean that we don't have it nicely washed and vacuumed!

How about dressing as a prop in the sales call?

Today's business environment is much more casual, there is no doubt about that. However, that creates an ambiguity we have never had before but also a unique opportunity.

It was easier when the expectation was suit and tie and pocket handkerchief; that was the dress of the professional salesperson. Now the tie has disappeared and we have degrees of business casual. Here is where there is an opportunity…

The opportunity is for differentiation, to create a personal brand to show the world. Think for a moment how you want to be seen and create the "package" that reflects that in your dress.

At our monthly Trusted Advisor Selling Institute, we had a gentleman who dressed in different coloured jackets and matching shoes each month; he always created an impact when he walked into the room.

Cufflinks and tailored shirts create a difference, as do shiny shoes and a well-pressed suit or jacket. Some things don't change. How about accessories? Take the pen, the satchel, or briefcase, for example.

The Mont Blanc pen might be a $500 investment, but it is one of the most used accessory of the trusted advisor salesperson. Each day you need to use your pen, to make notes on an appointment, to sign a contract or proposal. Stylish, refillable, and makes a statement when you rest it on your notepad. It says, "I believe in quality, I believe in investing in myself and I only like the best." Senior decision makers in the "C-Suite" will notice as they most likely will also have a pen of the same calibre.

A leather satchel or briefcase to house your notepad and perhaps an iPad can be a good $300 to $400 investment.

Again, it will be used for every appointment, every time you use theatre in your first meeting. Much better than asking your prospect for some paper or writing a note or two on the back of an old brochure. Or worse yet, not making notes at all.

Don't underestimate the impression of the theatre in the first two minutes by setting the stage for success and managing your props to create congruence with your message.

Write and Rehearse Your Script

The theatre of the sale requires a script.

You need to (at least) jot down an outline of what you are going to present and how you plan to improvise. Rehearse all likely variations.

Run through the questions that the customer might ask and the types of responses you'll make if those questions come up.

Great salespeople think through these alternatives. They also conduct role plays with their team. How else are they going to stay ready to take on all variations of their theme?

Map out the path your sales process is likely to traverse, starting with the initial rapport building all the way to the close. For a new piece of business, your average meeting might be 30-60 minutes.

And, if you're not selling a highly technical, high-investment type product or service, you may be able to make the sale on the day.

Toss around in your mind the alternative ways that you might test the water to find out whether your buyer is hot or cold. The value of 10 minutes spent in the car or at your desk prior to the appointment researching can't be overlooked.

The value of LinkedIn is huge—it gives you their whole work, clubs they belong to and schools they went to if populated correctly in their profile. Read through your script to remind yourself what sort of things you'll need to be saying to remind yourself of the triggers and those all-important LINKS that get you from A to B, B to C, C to D, etc., to tell your story.

It doesn't have to be scripted down to the word. What we are trying to do is to get into flow, and a series of bullet points you can re-visit prior to the meeting works for me. So what might be a good structure to script your presentation around? I have found a simple structure has always worked for me.

The script should contain:

- Your opening rapport builder, observation made in reception, etc.
- Your segue into the intelligent opening question
- Three quick questions to uncover wants and needs
- Stories that may be used
- Your segue to the demonstration phase of the appointment
- Your recommendations as to "where to go from here"
- The next steps…

A number of these steps are covered under the various techniques and ideas covered in the second part of this book.

The Value of "What's New"?

When I was selling our corporate range of diaries in a past life, I knew one of the favourite questions my buyers would ask was "what's new?" We would call on our clients each year at about the same time as well and not a great deal changed in the diary industry in terms of styles and finishes, so to be able to talk about a new cover or layout was of great help.

In fact, theatre could also be created by mentioning that something was new even if it wasn't "hot off the press," and this could be achieved by noting after the sales appointment exactly the products you demonstrated to each account in the

CRM system.

My biggest client was a Sydney-based national stationary company with multiple locations and I usually had about 20 minutes with them each year to review the previous year's "sell through" of the range and then to present what I thought would be great additional lines.

The decision maker would simply ask each year at the appropriate time, 'So Brad, what's new?'

You had about five minutes to cover anything you felt might work well for them and that was it… no more opportunity until the following year at the same time. Now that's when you need a script, a plan of what you are going to cover and how you will cover it. Samples, pricing sheets, features and benefit statements all ready.

What you and your customer call "news" isn't going to appeal to everyone. You would have to be in that line of business to be interested, but if you are in that game, if it's new, it would have to be interesting. Unless your product has a red-hot news angle, you probably won't find what you need on the mainstream media, so you might have to track your news online, through trade magazines or by word-of-mouth. Maybe, as it was for me, it's internal news, like something that's going on within the trade.

A new product, a new range, a new colour or even the way

the product is presented. Although new is the best way to lead, it has to stay abreast with the times. You can almost certainly re-use the rest of your script, but news always has a use-by date, that's what makes it new. One of your duties is to stay tuned to your market.

The script is your sales presentation—make a note of great questions that get a response, remember the main points and pillars of uniqueness in your strategic message of uniqueness.

Like great theatre, the script contains the roadmap for the language and the emphasis. It is also the outline for the joint presentation where both salespeople know their roles or when the sales manager accompanies you on a sales call. Think about your script and allow flexibility to improvise when the moment takes you and you are totally present.

So can the script allow for deviations? I mean, we can hardly ask the buyer to play their role and be a perfect customer or prospect and allow us to keep on track with exactly what we want to cover. In fact, some of most skilled buyers I have met are experts at throwing the salesperson off course in a highly competitive bid.

Your script should allow all sorts of variations, depending on whom you're talking to. You need to be flexible and the questions must flow from being present with what you are hearing from the buyer. This is where active listening comes into it. It's like being the interviewer of a special guest on my monthly video podcast. When I started doing the interviews, I wrote out all of my questions in advance and then went from one to the next.

The only problem with this method is that it's easy for you not to be in sync with the guest as you haven't followed on from their last answer, and I think the listener picks up on it. The guests invariably have something really interesting to say and when you are 100 percent present with them, your next questions simply flow from the conversation.

A number of people I have met in business talk about "wordtracks"—a script of the conversation you are about to have with a flowchart of the questions you are to ask in the event of a yes or no reply.

These are common in telemarketing sales when the operator could be changed every couple of hours and someone else takes over on behalf of the company who is hiring them.

As much as we always teach a customised dialogue approach in our selling methods, this process can create quality of approach by trying different words and tonality and then the script being changed accordingly to improve the response or conversion rate as time goes on.

As a good deal of my conversation in this book revolves around face-to-face selling and in a business-to-business environment, I haven't expanded on this.

I have always found it really helpful when I deliver my sales presentation to listen and watch the reaction to certain words and phrases and when I can see one word or phrase gets a reaction, I make a note in my journal as soon as I get to the car so I don't forget.

In the speaking industry, we know that the use of a word and the tone and speed of delivery of that word or phrase can make all the difference in prompting a laugh at the prescribed time. It's funny, but sometimes when you don't hit the word or phrase with exactly the right emphasis, it can go flat, and yet you might have said it slightly differently the previous day and it worked a treat!

The other technique used on the platform is what we call a "call back." This is when we go back to a phrase we have previously used in the presentation and repeat it again and perhaps not event finish the phrase and let the audience fill in the gaps.

Powerful approach when you get them reciting it back to you word for word; it provides evidence to the power of your message.

Be with the buyer 100 percent, have a script as to where you are going, but make the process flexible.

Some of the stories, soundbites, and other aspects of the presentation will be reusable time and time again. So it's worth learning your script as well as you can. You'll be using that script more than once. Put on the mask, remember your script, and walk on stage.

Part B

Bringing the Theatre to Life

How **Trusted Advisors** Create Sales Experiences and Not Just Sales Calls

Sales Experiences and Not Just Sales Calls

So we have set the scene for the theatre of the sale.

In this section, we explore the ways we can punctuate the sales experience with a number of cameos and vignettes.

It's a collection of 25 simple and yet powerful and effective ideas and tactics to make your theatre come to life.

Not all these ideas are mine.

They are an accumulation of experiences I have either used first-hand or observed while on many sales calls over the last 30 years with brilliant and accomplished trusted advisor salespeople.

The magic of each idea is in the implementation and delivery of the technique.

Trusted advisors make this a lifelong learning journey as they understand you never become a master of everything in sales but that you commit to continuous and never-ending improvement.

Some of the concepts explained are in fact from the golden days of selling when my dad was in his prime selling electrical appliances. He would share the importance of a technique when we did sales calls together early in my sales career.

When I share a number of these techniques with my members at the Trusted Advisor Selling Institute, members have their own favourite one and can't wait to leave the room and get to work on using it on their next sales call.

I could have written more as there are so many ways to put real theatre and showmanship into the sale, but then it would give you more to apply. Don't underestimate the value of an idea—some of these methods of theatre have literally made me hundreds of thousands of dollars.

This is the raw essence of selling—it's where the rubber hits the road, the concepts become a reality and you can apply them immediately.

Have fun and I would love to hear what works for you.

The Frame-Up—Defining the Situation

The "Frame Up" sounds like something in an art gallery. In a way, it is. I'm suggesting you place a frame around the whole interaction so all parties know what's going on and where they stand. It defines the situation and, having done that, allows both parties to prepare for the role each is about to play. Buyers have to prepare their, "Oh, I'm really interested in your product" face and you've got to entertain, teach, and close.

As I said, start by getting your client to agree to a definition of the situation. Make it clear that this call is not just social—buyers don't have time for that now. Frame the call in a sales context. Before you proceed, the other party should acknowledge that.

Putting the reason for the meeting in a frame grants you permission to move into areas that normally might be seen as overstepping the mark.

For example, to "make this solution worth for you," the salesperson might have to enquire about the buyer's budgetary expectations. That's usually private but not if you've contextualized your meeting. Their buying constraints are useful to know.

Face-to-face with buyers requires a context. After all, you didn't deal with cross-town traffic just for a coffee and a chat.

Getting agreement at this point as to your purpose means you can focus on storytelling, soundbites, models, visuals, analogies and everything else you have so conscientiously prepared.

The Outer Frame

Capture their attention within the first 30 seconds and get their tacit acceptance about what ground you would like to cover. It goes something like this:

'Mr./Ms. Jones, this is what I thought we would cover today…'

Or,

'Today is somewhat exploratory. I thought it would be great

to find out more about your business and then I can show you about our offering and we can find out whether there's a good fit between us to move forward. Is that okay with you?'

Or how about,

'I've researched your company online and I couldn't help but notice...'

These words frame up the conversation that you're about to have and shows you are not in the business of wasting your buyers' time. In fact, on occasion I have even started with that exact statement:

'I am not in the business of wasting people's time and I really appreciate you taking this meeting today...'

Backing this statement with a timeframe you have allowed for works extremely well, such as, **'We had planned for about 45 minutes for today's meeting. Is that timeframe okay with you?'**

The reason why you want to find this out is so you don't have that situation where the buyer halfway through the meeting starts to look at their watch and cut your timeframe shorter. Things happen in business and you may not be the highest priority to the buyer right there and then, so let's get the timeframe nailed down. If we don't get the outer frame established, I have noticed when coaching salespeople that they tend to speed up the presentation to get through all the points they wanted to make and this is ineffective.

If it happens, leave something out but don't change the pace. Remember, your buyer doesn't know your script and what you are planning to say, so only you will know that you deliberately left something out.

I have a client who sells a range of products in the pharmacy trade. The decision-making authority lies in many cases with the pharmacy manager and not the pharmacist. They endeavour to always get to see the pharmacy manager first before they re-stock the displays.

They set up the frame at the beginning of the visit and let the manager know in advance that they have some new things to show the manager and get their opinion before they leave. Now they have set themselves up for a really meaningful customer experience.

***Once you have established the outer frame of the meeting purpose, then it's time for the** inner frame.*

The Inner Frame

This is an unwritten agenda about what you intend to cover in this appointment. The inner frame is a summary statement on the back of the first statement in the outer frame.

It goes something like this:

'Bill, so I have some questions for you today to better understand your current requirements and where we might be able to add value. I then would love to introduce you to our solution and to see if we fit with the requirements.'

Perhaps if you are going back for the second appointment, you could take this approach: **'I have brought with me the pricing we spoke about as well and we can go through that. If it then makes sense to you to see how the machine operates, I will organise the demonstration at our showroom with our technical advisor while I am here and we can pop it into the diary. How does that sound to you?'**

I can't emphasise enough the value of getting their agreement at this point as it cements the frame up of the sales call and gives you permission to proceed. It also says to the buyer that if I can fulfil my promise by professionally showing you the range of the pricing schedule, then you need to fulfil yours with granting me the next steps in the sales process.

Both the outer and inner frame of the sales customer experience shows you to be a true trusted advisor, someone who is prepared, time focused, someone who values the opportunity, and it gives them a sneak glimpse of what they can expect from you should you be successful.

Great Theatre of the Sale Tip:

Try framing up your customer experiences and script it to get comfortable with the process, and you will notice a much higher level of engagement, more rapport, and generally a much better flowing interaction which will make perfect sense to the client.

Emotion Beats Logic

Your first job is to capture interest.

Your second will be to teach what the customer needs to know to feel confident about going ahead with the purchase, and your third will transform your role into a problem-solver and solution-finder before you confirm the sale.

Beginning this process is not difficult. Simply create the right question and customers will pour out their challenges if you know they aren't happy with a current provider.

If they are generally happy with the incumbent, it's a little more difficult. You have to challenge and tease out a better desired state than what they are currently experiencing.

Ask questions, challenge their thinking, and don't be afraid to be cheeky if you have developed good, solid rapport. It's amazing how many buyers really appreciate a sophisticated trusted advisor who has provocative questions that change the game.

Remember, people love talking. Your best response is to listen, while getting your bearings.

All early sales texts will tell you that people justify their purchases with logic but buy with their emotions. In broad terms I agree with this and have seen it work first-hand. Get the balance right - with the logic of the purchase while understanding the customer's emotions, so pay attention to the environment you are in and the message your buyer is giving off.

Emotion is a powerful thing; it's amazing how this will influence the buying process, especially when the buyer really wants what you have.

There are plenty of logical reasons why buyers buy. Maybe to increase margins, lower costs, provide more efficiency, increase market share, gain a competitive advantage, to service key performance indicators (KPIs), or you may simply have passed their price comparison test.

These are all "reasons to buy," but they are not as strong as looking good in front of their boss, making their life easier, or reducing their stress.

For example, price comparison makes them look good, allowing them to report to their sales manager that they made a purchase that saves the company money. Despite the logic of the purchase, the real reason is that they may have simply bought themselves a promotion.

People have many emotional drivers, different strokes for different folks. Maslow's famous Hierarchy of Needs states our core drivers are security needs, but this society is way beyond that. More significantly, we have self-actualisation needs.

Pride of ownership is one example. Consider the car industry. ("Sell the smell while raving about the saving.") When your customers realise they can actually own that prestige car (with the smell of the leather and the feel of the wheel), they're probably hooked! These sensory pleasures engage them to make what they will later describe to their sales boss as the 'only logical purchase under the circumstances.'

When I bought my last car, an XF Jaguar, I received from the salesperson a classic "six position walk around" as they are trained in the car and truck industry.

If you don't know what that is, in a nutshell, the salesperson takes you around the car and points out each feature and the benefit of that feature to you. If they are good, they will ask along the way 'how important is that to you?' or, 'what do you think of that?'

These were all logical reasons to buy the car. In my case with the Jaguar, it took them a while to really work out who they were speaking to. They had a non-technical but highly emotive buyer who just liked the look of the car. It really wasn't until we got into the car that he shifted the conversation into what I did for a career and what attracted me to the car in the first place.

I must admit, I was sold probably before I even reached the car yard because I loved the shape and look of the car and I wanted a sporty looking car which had four doors and allowed me to transport our young family. It was really the only model I had found that would work, so it just came down to the monthly repayment and the business manager working his magic with the rates and balloon payment at the end.

You get a sense when you are in sales for a while as to what really drives the buyer and when there are two very closely aligned products with similar features and benefits, it will come down to personal preference and their emotive response.

To be absolutely candid, I think I was calculating the per-month lease payments while he was chatting me while doing the test drive!

To sell prestige items, salespeople have to present themselves as being special too. They dress resplendently because they know they can't sell a prestige item if they're wearing overalls. The more prestigious the item, the more theatrical the sale must be.

Taking the item out of a glass cabinet and holding it delicately with a gloved hand talks up the sale without saying a word. If pride and prestige were unimportant, Montblanc would never sell their $500 pens when perfectly good $2 pens can be bought from any newsagency.

Whom is your client trying to impress? Play to that imaginary audience. No customer is going to admit s/he is making the purchase in order to improve their personal standing in the company. Who admits to that? Who admits to peer pressure? No one. It's up to you to scratch that surface.

Read the situation and play the appropriate role. And, salespeople read situations by being observant. There are clues all over the place—signifiers, I call them. Remember, the customer is playing a role too. Over the years, s/he has developed a persona that handles their role—their job—with conviction.

Despite the title on their office door and business card, they are not really a Branch Manager, Customer Relations Officer, or whatever. They are a parent, a partner, a club member, etc., and they have put aside their other selves to play this role to advance their personal goals. Clues about their real selves are all around if you look. Sometimes they are hung on a wall or displayed on their desk. Nowadays they are even tattooed on their skin, depicting motorbikes, plants, names, pets, religious symbols, gargoyles, sporting logos and so on.

Times have changed. A web designer for a major media firm has tattoos of eucalypt leaves on her upper arms. When asked why, she'll tell you all about her childhood. This information has to be useful, if for no other reason than as an icebreaker, until you move the conversation.

In *Life's a Pitch*, Broughton states that "selling is about understanding a customer's needs and delivering a product to meet them." Three pieces he describes as being key: economic, structural, and psychological.

It's amazing how many buyers will find the money when they really want the product or the solution you are offering. In my experience, it's all about what your solution will do for them and how many times over they can gain a benefit from using you.

Emotion has a good deal to do with what the buyer can gain from working with you to make their life better. It could be that your solution will make them look good in front of their team, help them secure that next promotion, save their department money, which in turn makes the buyer look responsible, or even promote the company name or brand in the market.

When I started in sales, I was always told to look out for the "buying signals," those verbal and non-verbal clues that a buyer leaves. But you need to be observant. I am amazed how many times I've sat beside a salesperson on a sales call when coaching in the field and the salesperson misses the clue and continues talking and explaining an irrelevant feature of the product or solution.

These triggers come in different shapes and forms—it could be something as simple as them leaning forward when you are explaining the product or making a note of the investment on the front page of the proposal and scribbling down things like monthly repayments. Perhaps holding the sample in their hands (for example, leather diaries always got a reaction, people always love the smell and feel of the leather!).

Most of the emotional triggers I find come in the facial expressions and the questions they ask. We need to be on our "A game" to notice these things.

Nodding at you while you talk about your competitive advantage or a smile when you both know your solution is in the ballpark of what they discussed was their budget in the first meeting. A highly emotional state is the perfect time to ask for a commitment, so don't be afraid to ask for a YES when you can sense it.

Think for a moment of an opportunity for you to make the buyer look good or how you can flatter the ego by helping them to make an informed decision.

Great Theatre of the Sale Tip:

Be present, be aware, and spend a good deal of time watching your client, learning responses to their questions, and enhancing your response and presentation. Don't miss the signals!

The Power of Scarcity

A good sales presentation begins by grabbing the attention of the customer, "arousing interest" or however you want to word it. You grab the attention of your customers or prospects by the way you act and by what you say. It's actually all you've got. One way to capture buyer interest is by accentuating your positives. The trusted advisor approach is never ever about lying to the customer, but never under-estimate the power of scarce resources.

We want it more when it's scarce. Buyers exaggerate the worth of the item if it seems in short supply.

This makes the product seem in-demand and a little bit mysterious, with just a hint of the suggestion that it might not be available again.

Scarcity sells and the salesperson's role is to drive that need. As salespeople, we have the opportunity right here of injecting a bit of drama. Dance with the script, make your offer more challenging, work with the tension of "less," of "only available in a few colours," "only available in this size," "only available if you can get the order to me today"—that's your message.

Being the first person to own one carries the same mystique. That's why we have people camping out when Microsoft releases the new Windows software or when bookshops take stock of the latest Harry Potter novel.

Many years ago, I did some work for a Telecommunications provider who had a number of retail stores with a young sales team. One of my students sold phone accessories and brightly coloured phone covers. That was her job. After the first sales training session, she said to me, 'Your idea of scarcity is working for me a treat, the pink ones sell pretty well!'

'Explain?' I asked. She continued, 'I have found that if I take a few pink ones off the stand; it makes them seem scarcer.'

I then fired back, 'So you have them in short supply then?'

To which she replied, 'Nah, we've got boxes of them in the warehouse.'

That's right—creating a sense of scarcity helped move her stock. I let her know that it wasn't really the point I was making and I am not sure her manager wanted to hear that. If they are an experienced retailer at that franchise, I am guessing they may have subscribed to the old retail adage of "stack 'em high and watch 'em buy" from the stationery trade days.

The same applies when selling cars, coats, camping gear, houses, and everything else. If you don't have many of them, they automatically become in more demand. For example, when you're buying a house, you want a certain outlook, a number of bedrooms, a certain type of backyard and pool—and no one wants to risk missing out. The more they want something, the more they'll climb over hot coals to get it.

Real estate salespeople are experts at this. When courting you for listing, there is a standard part of their presentation where they will show you that there are "no other houses around like yours right now and we have so many buyers out there." Amazing how after say –three to four months and the agent opening the house up for inspection that they obviously didn't want your house though?

It's also a selling strategy for the agent to liaise on the other side of the fence with the buyer and talk about how s/he "just doesn't have anything else like this at the moment so you don't want to miss out!"

Once you see yourself in the property and are emotionally connected to it, half the sale is made. Classic scarcity selling.

Scarcity selling is similar to dating. Think of the thrill of the chase you had when you were courting your loved one, the flutter of the heart when it was revealed they felt the same way about you. A phone with no left message is cruel scarcity selling!

So how important is real scarcity versus fake scarcity?

Well, I think as trusted advisors our goal is to make repeated sales and develop relationships for life and so transparency and authenticity is a high priority at all times in the selling process.

Buyers will always appreciate trust, as so many before you have not always acted with such integrity.

Saying 'I am not sure how long this one will be in our warehouse' or 'I am not sure based on this month's demand how many of them we will have by mid-July' is fine. It's not lying at all.

You see, we don't actually know what the outcome will be at the end of the month for the stockholding of an item, we are only making a guess. However, going back to my last example at the telecommunications store saying that this is the last one and then refilling the stand five minutes later and creating a new "last one" is asking for trouble!

How is YOUR performance?

You don't want to lose customers by making purchase of the product seem inconvenient, or worse, appearing to be aloof. You **do** want to generate excitement in the purchase. It can be done by making it seem special and a little bit scarce. When you have something you know is going to be in high demand, value it.

Great Theatre of the Sale Tip:

Selling scarcity is all about putting doubt in the mind of the buyer. Doubt that there may not be another one or perhaps doubt about your availability and workload and current clients you work with if you are a trusted advisor in the service profession.

The Magic of Storytelling

Storytelling is a powerful way of capturing interest and holding it.

Interest isn't the only thing you're holding in the palm of your hand. You are also holding—and withholding—important information. So mete it out appropriately and enticingly.

I have already made clear my preference for face-to-face selling. Storytelling is another difference between you and a website. You are vibrant, on their premises, and you've got an interesting routine. Clients love hearing stories, tales, yarns, gossip, and news. They love being entertained.

The simplest example comes from one of my former

customers who was an "anchor account" when I was in the diary business. We would always call a customer who provided great sales volumes of a style of product an "anchor account", as they allowed us to increase our quantities and then sell the product to other markets as well.

I'd regularly visit this customer and he'd always go through the same routine. He'd brush all production and financial details aside, look me up and down, and say, 'Tell me something new.' I would. After that, our business was usually over and done in 20 minutes, which is remarkably fast when you total the size of the transaction.

Something new is not about reeling off a stack of numbers; it's about presenting a new solution with a story of how the product could be used.

Each story is like a module within the larger context of your presentation. It can be used or not used, depending on whether or not it adds to this particular session.

Each story should lead to an object lesson at its close. Its beginning draws listeners in, its middle expands the proposition, and its conclusion is the "therefore bit" that points out the message.

Your story is a clear example that personifies your product.

Sometimes it resolves in a call-to–action, but that isn't always necessary. The call-to-action may follow later, after you've covered more ground.

I suggest creating stories as self-contained vignettes. Although you will try to make each story seem spontaneous, they can be well rehearsed and used whenever required to amplify a point you are making. You may have 20 of these up your sleeve, each one a simple, illustrative example of where you want your sales presentation to go.

Have you ever watched Billy Connolly tell an anecdote? He's fantastic, isn't he? The way he gets you so engrossed. He makes it look as if the tale just came to him right there, on stage, in the middle of talking about something else. The truth is that every story is well crafted.

They are designed to totally engage the audience. (We know this because he often does the same routine the following night).

In telling his story, sometimes he pauses midway, as if he's forgotten what he was talking about, then he talks about something else and returns to it later.

That's called "closing an open loop," the ability to get people involved, leave them hanging, come back, wrap up the tale, and deliver the punchline.

You can see the look on the audience face when he goes

back to the story later on in the night; they have that quizzical nature about them where they just realised they didn't get a conclusion to the tale.

How about the growth of TED.com? You can go onto TED.com and listen to a 15-minute story. The person doing the story telling is relating one simple story and it's an online success because we love them. Why? Because:

1. Stories build social proof and credibility.
2. Stories put customers in the picture.
3. Stories are visual, auditory, and kinaesthetic.

Telling stories as selling vehicles enable you to get the present customer to identify with the buyer in the story. Relate how things worked out positively.

Resolve the story with a winning result.

To make stories work in a sales context, you need four things:

1. A character (the client),
2. A problem,
3. Your expertise, and
4. A successful result.

Many years ago, I was selling compendiums, i.e., writing folders with mock-leather or leather covers. I called on a lady named Kay who wanted the less expensive model, i.e., a PVC or a vinyl compendium. Even so, I thought I should bring a leather one in my bag, just in case. After settling in, I started talking about materials other than leather, the cheaper ones, which is where she wanted the conversation to go.

Then I told her the story of Nappa leather, the softest, most beautiful leather you can get in our range. The tale involved a character, a problem, and a satisfactory conclusion, and I made her laugh, which is always a good sign.

I asked her to visualise a connection between the leather compendium and a cow and I wrapped the story up with, 'If the compendium has an imperfection in the leather, it's simply because the cow sat on the fence!'

I'm no Billy Connolly, but that little cow story made her chuckle, which enabled me to upsell her a $130 compendium over a cheaper vinyl one.

I guess I dramatised it a bit by producing the leather one from my briefcase and smelling it. It smelt enticing, leather always does. I passed it across and she smelt it too. People love smelling leather.

Your Back Story

The prior life of the character is the back story.

In *Intent to Live*, Larry Moss shows us a deep understanding of the inner workings of acting and his experience in working with some of Hollywood's leading actors. He talks about how the back story is vital in letting the character unfold in front of the audience. He describes the back story as the series of events that propelled them to where they are.

In selling, it is up to us to develop the credibility in front of the buyer. One of the most effective ways to achieve this is by a story about our experience in the field. To be able to briefly tell our buyer our experience and how that experience will be of great help to them to making this decision in front of them.

We all have years of experience and countless customers we have helped by recommending a solution. We just need to tap into this.

When I was working with John Deere in agricultural sales, those salespeople who came from a technician background were at an advantage over the other sales professionals. Farmers were happy to see them and talk about the machinery. They had the credibility and they knew what the machinery could do as well as how to fix it. I saw first-hand the benefit of being able to talk the language of the farmer and share a story, whether it be about the piece of machinery or even the weather and the crop forecast for that season.

A story humanises the discussion—it makes it personal and

not just a sales call filled with features and benefits. We all have stories, plenty of them. The problem is that we don't think anyone would want to listen to them.

It's a common misconception when I am working with salespeople one to one that they have overlooked this tactical piece of theatre.

The other great thing about storytelling when you are a member of a sales team is that the stories in the company can be shared and be the property of the team by using the "royal we." Saying something like, 'We had a client who…' or, 'one of our customers…' is really powerful stuff.

A story doesn't have to be long–winded; it can be a short example. A good friend of mine, Lou Heckler CPAE in Florida, a speaker coach, calls the shorter stories "vignettes."

You may use a number of these shorter examples through a sales appointment. Lou has always said to me that you need to have a number of these vignettes and stories in your toolbox and to bring them out on each appointment. He is also very passionate about the fact that we should be rehearsing them and getting great at telling them by using the same stories with a variety of clients in sales.

Great storytelling needs to be rehearsed to make sure the main point is clear to the buyer or it just becomes a self-serving yarn and business really doesn't have a lot of time for that these days. So start thinking of customer challenges, how you solved them, and the customers who experienced that solution.

Ask them for their permission to use their name or company. Bring a testimonial or referral to life by having a client make a recommendation of you on the phone to a prospective new client.

Great stories include colour, they need detail to come to life. As my speaking coach Lou told me, a story gives a "sneak peek" behind the curtain to a part of you that may not usually see. The road to closing a sale begins with gaining attention, and a good story will always do that.

Great Theatre of the Sale Tip:

Make a list now of your stories, the people you have helped over the years, and how they have become trusted friends. Use the formula I gave before—a client, a challenge they faced, and how you offered a solution, and then hey, presto! A successful result!

The Soundbite

In a meeting of two parties, conversations comprise of a series of "points" where one party makes brief affirmations that they understand what is being said. The other part of the conversation comprises a number of short "presentations" where one party expresses something which is bounced back and forth. This chapter is about the first part, the points.

"Points" can be little more than nonsensical expressions, not always found in the dictionary, like 'uh huh' and 'mm.' Other times, they are real words, like "yep" and "go on…"

They may even be a restatement of what has been said, to affirm that the hearer has understood and is on the same track. It sometimes goes like this:

'Leather?'

'Yes, leather.'

'Go on.'

It may not sound very clever, but that's how we talk. Salespeople don't have to leave it at that. They can make more of this without applying a brake on what the speaker is saying. You can often inject brief messages into those points. I call them "soundbites." Unlike "mm" and "uh-huh," they are short, punchy phrases that you will find in the dictionary. They advance your cause because after you've repeated them a few times, they stick in the listeners' minds.

Soundbites are short statements as used by the media and politicians to sell their message. They are sometimes called catchphrases.

One such catchphrase that the Liberal Party of Australia kept repeating when they were trying to get Tony Abbott elected was "stop the boats." Having said that seemingly absolved them from explaining all practicality of what they said. They turned themselves into the "Stop the Boats" Party, and by inference, the other parties wouldn't or couldn't do that.

Another example is former US president Ronald Reagan. His "win one for the gipper" became a very famous soundbite.

I don't even know what "the gipper" is—do you? But Reagan used that phrase to very good advantage because whenever he said it, everybody cheered as if he'd said something clever.

Donald Trump injected the word "crooked" to poison the waters. Every time he named Hillary Clinton, he called her Crooked Hillary. He did it so frequently that every time his audience heard the name Hillary, they subconsciously thought "crooked." That was the whole idea.

No further justification was required. I didn't say soundbites were necessarily fair. In fact, like the "gipper," they can be a little bit silly. But simple messages repeated over and over again lock themselves into people's subconscious.

The best policy is to:

(1) Say it,

(2) Explain it, and

(3) Repeat it.

But don't keep explaining it. The purpose of the soundbite is to avoid doing that. You may be sharing a complex message—like a specification—and simplifying it makes it memorable until it locks in as a truism.

My soundbite is "trusted advisor selling." If I'm visiting a prospect, I want them to remember that I am the "trusted advisor selling" guy.

I might use the words "trusted advisor" dozens of times during my one-day program as I truly believe that we develop a great sales business by being that advisor that people trust.

I want that catchphrase to be remembered and I know that repetition works. You may recall the simple maxim: "tell 'em and tell 'em and tell 'em." I believe that.

Here's another soundbite. This one is (or was) used by McDonald's in their customer service training: 'Two deep is too deep,' said when referring to the lines at their fast restaurants. If you've heard it for the tenth time, you probably want to strangle the person who's saying it. But the first time you hear it, it sticks.

Chances are your customers are going to forget 90 percent of whatever you tell them. However, they do remember soundbites and other snappy reference points.

Great selling is all about having them remember you, your product or solution, and what it can do for them.

I don't want to be "vanilla" sales guy (i.e., just like anyone else), I want to be Neapolitan, with some shades of personality.

The professional speaking industry defines the soundbites we use as "call backs," a way to remember the key catchphrase of the presentation after a 45, 60, or 90-minute keynote.

After a presentation, we know that an audience will only remember a percentage of what you tell them. That's human nature and based on our ability to keep our concentration for extended periods.

So to have people all milling around at the coffee station outside the conference room after your keynote reciting the "call back" you used to capture their attention means that you are leaving a lasting legacy from the speech.

To accentuate the power of a soundbite in a sales presentation, don't overlook repeating it back to the customer or prospect for effect, using a pause to build up the anticipation.

Practice has shown me that an initial soundbite with a couple of repeats in a 60-minute meeting is very achievable.

Brainstorm the product range and solution and think about your unique offering, or perhaps look at your competitive advantage in the market and come up with something that you and the team can all use to land the punch when making your point either in a sales presentation or a casual chat with a customer.

Think also about the application of the idea when you are asked to do an interview on a podcast or write an industry article or perhaps a blog post you might like to start—all great opportunities to use the soundbite.

Great Theatre of the Sale Tip:

Develop a catch phrase that reinforces your memorable point. Think of a competitive advantage in the market—the things that you stand for—and create one line catchphrases you can use in your meetings. Then reinforce them in the written form when you send back a note or a proposal.

The Principle of Ingratiation

This chapter is about genuinely saying something nice to the buyer. Listen and discover something you admire about them and then deliver with sincerity.

Buyers are already cynical. They've seen all the sales techniques lampooned and exposed on TV. They've probably read "how to sell" magazine articles. They may even be salespeople themselves, so they know all the "tricks." It must be time to mean what you say.

The principle of ingratiation has little room for theatre. You have to mean it. All of us like to bask in a little bit of praise now and then. If it's a nice photo on the wall, say so. If it's a good coffee, say so. If they make a good product, tell them.

But what I am suggesting here is much more than that.

Note in press conferences, celebrities often preface their responses with, 'That's an excellent question…'

Why do they say this?

First, it puts the questioner at ease. Second, it creates a little pause between question and answer so they can collect their thoughts.

As a great listener and engaging trusted sales advisor, you can use that approach too:

'That's a really interesting perspective… or, 'I haven't been asked that question in a long time, that's a spot-on observation.' Does it have to be a "really interesting perspective"? Not necessarily.

You see, in sales we get asked the same sorts of questions on an ongoing basis and that's okay. It may be the seventh time you have been asked that exact question this week, and this is where the theatre comes in.

But remember, this is the first time that the customer sitting in front of you has asked you that particular question.

Honour it, respect it, and don't downplay it!

The customer or prospect has no idea how many times you have been asked that question; they don't sell what you sell. Business owners appreciate it when you have noticed that they have done an amazing job at building a great business. Let's face it, it's not easy and takes discipline, risk taking, and long nights.

Remember that so many business owners (your prospects in so many businesses) attach a great percentage of their purpose in their success in business.

What an opportunity we have in the theatre of the sale to acknowledge their achievement, make them feel important, and also gain instant rapport. Ingratiation. If you look closely when you ingratiate your buyer, you can see a small smile or a look of pride on their face as they are instantaneously smarter people than what they were only five minutes ago, and you created that.

So how important is sincerity in delivering the ingratiation statement or acknowledgement of your buyer when sitting in front of them?

In one word, it's everything.

You see, when they really believe that you mean what you are saying, then the relationship in sales starts. You move in their eyes from the salesperson who just wants to make the sale to the trusted advisor who is there for the long haul.

When you say something like, 'That's an interesting perspective,' you don't want the buyer coming straight back with, 'WHY is it interesting? What makes it so interesting?'

If you don't mean it, you'll be lost for words. If you mean it, you would have a ready answer to that question.

Experienced salespeople will also have the follow-up statement ready as well. Something like, 'The reason I am saying that is because the more people I meet who have an interest in this model are not as curious with the mechanics of how the XC 9200 works.' Now you are flattering them by saying that they obviously have a keen and sophisticated mind with the technical aspects.

See how it works?

So … mean it or don't say it. It can't be impossible to smatter your conversation with expressions like, 'Nice car,' 'Smart thinking,' 'Nice one,' 'I'm glad you asked that,' 'Beautiful picture,' or words to that effect.

You must like or respect *something* about the prospect or why are you in sales in the first place? Remember, this is a people business.

Great Theatre of the Sale Tip:

Ingratiation is not a fake thing, it's real. It shows that you care about what people say to you; it says that you are listening intently and not just going on to the next thing. Take a moment and think of a soundbite, a short phrase that you would be comfortable to use in conversation to ingratiate your buyer and start using the phrase on every sales call and look for the opening. See what happens!

Proposal Foreplay

Proposal foreplay is real theatre—it plays to anticipation.

You've already (1) defined the meeting as a selling situation, (2) built the set, (3) separated your back-stage behaviour from front-stage, (4) developed the script, and (5) peppered whatever you plan to say with soundbites. It's now time to perform in earnest.

Do yourself a favour and watch some of the great stand-up performers. They use proposal foreplay in a big way. You think they've climaxed. The audience is rapt. Applause? Not quite, it's a dummy climax. The audience takes a backward step… is it now? Maybe not. Is it now? I'm not sure. Is it now?

Yes, it's now. Sold.

Maintaining control is absolutely essential. Engagement is perfect, and now it's time to maintain control of the unveiling.

Not only does the performer build the audience up, the performer holds the show together until s/he has received the desired response. I've seen performers repeat the joke if the audience didn't laugh first time around. That takes quite a bit of confidence, but it maintains control. Perhaps you have also noticed when a comedian has used a saving line like, 'Well, I won't use that joke again!'

Many years ago, I came across an experienced insurance salesperson at a networking function. We chatted about the fact that I had some investment properties that all needed to be insured ongoing, as well as my normal business, car, and contents insurance which was a yearly commitment.

He asked, 'Can I put a proposal together for you?' to which I said, 'Sure' (I mean, what the heck?). He was going to do all the work on my behalf and there was no guarantee of any business unless he was able to show savings!

We met one week later and discussed my requirements in detail, and then I gave him all the details he needed to draw comparisons with the current provider (I am a kind buyer!) to make his life easier. We agreed that it wouldn't be worthwhile if I couldn't see say a 10 to 15 percent difference in the current package price I was paying. This was the defined outcome for our next meeting.

Within the following week, we were to meet up again and he would outline what he had found out and what the proposal would look like.

So the next meeting was made in advance and we had another coffee. He had the proposal in his hands, and after pleasantries, we then moved into what his findings were. He proceeded to summarise the first meetings objectives like a great salesperson and what he thought his company could do for me. He did it while holding the proposal and tapping it with his fingers so I would not lose sight of the document.

As he tapped the folder, he started to tell me what was in the proposal and how much money he had been able to save me and the extra coverage he had achieved by using another insurer.

The whole time I kept thinking, "Gimme that folder!" But he proceeded to sell the proposal with words like, 'I've outlined how I can save you or around $300 a month.' As I kept thinking, "Gimme that folder!" he kept touching the proposal as he continued to talk.

"Gimme that folder!" The anticipation was killing me.

After what seemed an eternity, he finally handed over the proposal and then directed my attention to the bottom line on page 3, the savings. Very professionally executed, very professionally planned.

Anyway, he got my business. Of course he did!

So I couldn't help myself at the end of the meeting. He knew I was a coach of selling and someone who had a thirst for new ideas and concepts. I asked him about the theatre of keeping the document where I'd never lose sight of it, without him actually handing it over. He admitted this was all deliberate. He said, 'I learned this many years ago. It's called a pre-proposal.' Or, as I call it, 'proposal foreplay.'

So we sat there as two old sales experienced sales people telling tales about the days on the road talking with buyers about the power of the proposal foreplay.

One thing we know for sure is that when you hand a document to the buyer, or when you give them the data they want, their attention will switch onto the page before them and they'll stop listening to what you're telling them.

So don't hand that power over too early, retain the ball in your court.

While you hold the information they want, your buyer is susceptible to everything you say. Once handed over, their attention has shifted. I find the same thing when I pass out sales manuals or handouts to class members and I see their eyes all look down. It's hard to get them back for that brief moment.

Our objective with the theatre of the sale is to make an impact and to increase our chances of converting every sales opportunity. The insurance salesperson knew that the cost of that sales call to come and see me was an investment in many hours of work all up. So why not give yourself every chance of success!

We're not talking about delivering a soliloquy here. You may not need more than several 30-45-second bursts. Just build suspense. Entertain. Inform. Talk about benefits. Tell them stories. Underscore the research you've put into this.

Only pass the ball when you're ready.

How they catch it will tell you where they're at.

But wait, there's more. You haven't closed yet.

You've only sold the sizzle. The steak is what the document is about, but in reality, it just supports your argument.

Great Theatre of the Sale Tip:

Make sure you get the objective clear at the end of the first meeting in a multi-step sales process, go away and sculpture the proposal to achieve that objective, and then plan your proposal foreplay delivery. No more than 30-45 seconds is required, but it will add anticipation and excitement to your presentation.

Models and Process Visuals

There's a saying that pictures tell a thousand words. It might be time to let the pictures do the talking. Models and process visuals allow us to inject life into the pitch. They're like stage props. Keep them handy and be fluent in using them.

Models and process visuals will position you as someone to listen to, as long as they are relevant to where the buyer is right now and where they would like to head in the future.

I have a few visuals that I draw with a pen on paper in front of my buyers: pyramid shapes and circles done seemingly spontaneously to illustrate my points.

I've rehearsed how I present these on-the-spot drawings to increase professionalism, which is the first step on the road to becoming a trusted advisor.

A number of salespeople have asked me over the years whether you should have a number of these process visuals and models pre-prepared and laminated ready to go.

My answer is a resounding NO.

Part of the real theatre is to look like you've just thought of the idea and sketched it out in front of them. By the way, don't be surprised that they may ask you to keep that back of an envelope you sketched on as it may have had real cut through for them!

Earlier I wrote about what you "give" and what you "give off." Injecting a drawing, a picture, a graph, or a document into your presentation gives off a different vibe. It changes the rhythm of what's happening.

It also affects your positioning.

If you're hoping to create a friendly personal vibe, pen and paper will do that.

If you're coming across all corporate, there is a place to use professionally designed onscreen graphics.

Perhaps it's a four-quadrant diagram which can explain the different players in the industry or a three-circle diagram (as per below) explaining the different parts of your business and how they all operate in unison to help the customer.

Here are a couple of examples - the first one is the 4

quadrant diagram which can be unveiled to the customer by starting with labelling the 2 axis.

The great thing about the four-quadrant diagram (which comes from identifying two axis and naming them) is that it allows you to create avatars of the type of buyer or customer each quadrant represents.

This allows your customer to see themselves in the model and where they want to be aspirationally.

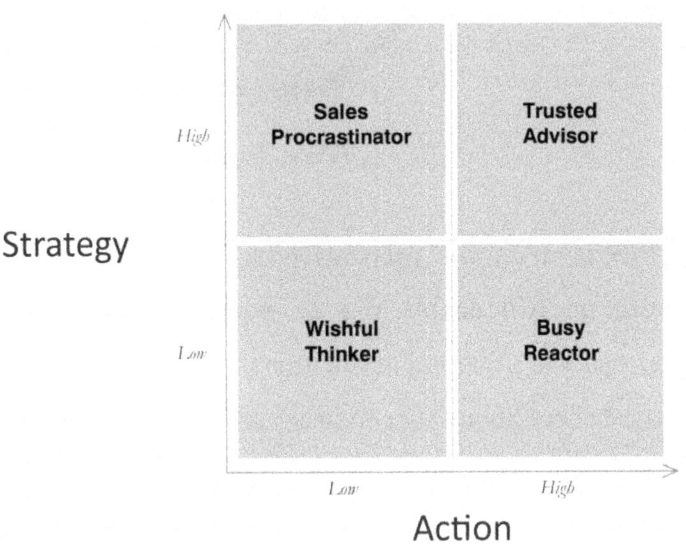

Four-quadrant diagram

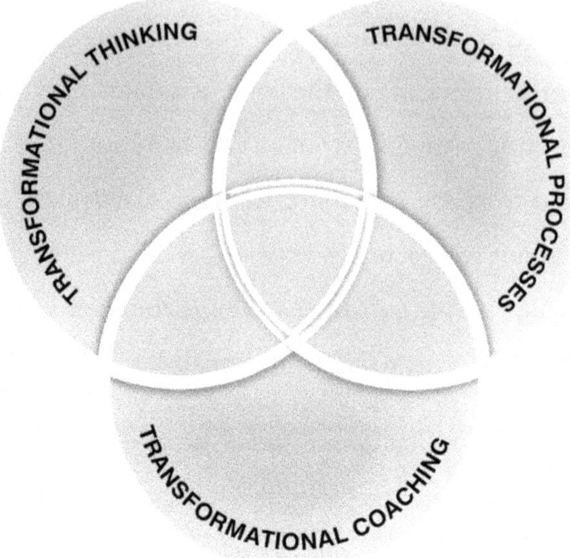

Venn diagram

Shown on the previous page, a well-constructed Venn diagram will enable you to explain to your customer or prospect in a fraction of the time how you are different or what you believe about your industry and/or the challenges of your customers. You can also allow them to give you feedback on a scale for each of the three aspects in the diagram as a diagnostic tool.

For example, if I was asking my customer to describe how much the transformational mindset might be a priority to them, they might label that as a 4 out of 5. If they saw the transformational coaching circle as being not as important they might label that as a 1.

A good friend and expert at developing and creating global digital empires, Chad Barr from the Chad Barr Group, has always said that the secret to great content is to make the content prolific and provocative. Models and process visuals allow you to do just that.

As we have said before, to stand out, your message has to be Neapolitan and not just vanilla. In designing your model and process visuals, you need to keep that in mind. How can what I depict give people a contrarian view to what else is out there? It doesn't have to be absolutely ground-breaking new, just a different view on an existing concept. Chad is the master of making an idea or concept come to life and he shows you how you can do it too.

Great process visuals and models create great theatre by:

- Being able to show your prospect your understanding of the industry and where you are most competitive by what segment you specialise in;
- Showing the prospect what problems you solve and how you solve them;
- Showing expertise, how you can on a piece of paper or whiteboard seemingly think of a solution to the client's problem and show them a way forward; and…

- Letting the other person know that they are not alone and that there is a proven solution which has worked before to solve this problem.

The aim is always to hold the buyer's attention by transmitting easily understood information. Create visuals that promote clarity. It's all part of your performance.

I want to emphasise a hand of cards without the ace. You can still win without it, but it's so much easier when you're playing it from your hand.

Great Theatre of the Sale Tip:

Think for a moment: what is something you can develop that you would be able to time and time again repeat to the buyer which shows your expertise?

The Message to Market

Your buyers may already have a vendor they are very happy with. Why should they switch to you? What is it about you that makes you different from the others? And why should s/he even consider your proposition? As a good friend of mine, Jim Pancero, says, 'The number one question in the buyer's mind is,

"Out of all the vendors available to me, why should I buy from you?"

Your answer could be: 'Because my product is unique.' But your product is NOT completely unique, that's the truth of it. Your "uniqueness" is entirely dependent on whether or not your performance succeeds in making the improbable appear believable. So elaborate and create a real niche of how your product has some exclusive benefits to the customer.

The answer to the question, "Why should I buy from you?" involves a type of rehearsal. It requires a dramatic realisation of your core message.

Your aim is to idealise this appointment and your product, to create in the buyer's mind an impression that this is indeed a fortuitous meeting. Only show the buyer the end product. Conceal all back-stage efforts to produce it. Present it as finished, polished, and packaged. High-end sportswear manufacturers show only the running shoes, never the sweatshop. As for "magic," all new age shops sell Tarot cards.

You don't get to see the print shop where they are waiting in line to get printed. By the time you see them, they are displayed amongst shrouds of incense so they adopt a mysterious dimension that wasn't there when they were uncut cardboard.

Here's another example of idealisation. Some years ago, I hired a well-known speaker who taught a daily session about nine types of difficult people. He had reduced all the problem people in the world to nine types. Why nine? Why not 11?

Why not 27? Answer: it was nine because he said so. That's all it was. His onstage performance idealised that number and he created a dramatic realisation that made it seem so. Simple.

Antiquarian booksellers are another good example of dramatic uniqueness. The shopfront doors are often closed with a sign that may say "By Appointment Only" so the customers feel privileged to be allowed inside.

The bookseller is invariably well dressed, handling the ancient books with great care, which is all part of the performance. The book itself—wonderful as it probably is—may have been found in a dusty attic somewhere. But here … it's unique.

Your performance is further enhanced by varying your vocal expression. Lowering your voice at a point of interest draws listeners in and raising it for emphasis lifts the climax of the story.

Now it's time for prepared spontaneity, a message to market. A one-line statement and a longer explanation about what makes you different.

So what makes a great message to market?

A message to market aims at identifying your uniqueness

and being able to transfer that uniqueness to the buyer so that it sticks!

1. **A one-line statement—a soundbite**—that you can use anywhere in a meeting that makes you and your solution unique.

   An example might be: 'We work with .... (target market) to .... (outcome) by our .... (process).'

2. **Three main pillars of uniqueness.** Create a brainstorm of ideas as to what you think makes your business and your offering unique.

   Don't worry if not everything is absolutely unique; it's the combination of the three things that creates a competitive position.

   Examples might be a more comprehensive product range, quality products and services, family-owned business, your account management structure, or perhaps the strength of the brand.

3. **Evidence and self-evident statements.** Back up your claim with evidence.

Presentation aids add credibility to this special moment. This could be demonstrations, testimonials, or endorsements.

An example of saying "our extensive product range" might be, 'We have over 210 models available in our range so we can provide one that fits your needs.'

I began this chapter by saying there is nothing unique about your product and I'm going to contradict myself by claiming that everything about you and your product is unique. In fact, THIS is a unique moment.

But… can the buyer see it and do they really care?

The real value of a great message to market is that we know through experience and talking with enough buyers in the market that what you are about to explain to them is going to be on the mark with the types of things they are looking for.

Of course, it's a great qualifier also. If you are giving your message to market to a potential buyer and they are not seeing value in what you are presenting to them about your point of difference, it will help to determine that you are not the right person for them but equally that they are not the ideal customer for you.

Remember, the art of great selling is to make sure we talk with enough of the right type of buyer and not just anyone with a "heartbeat and a wallet." So look for the reaction to what you are putting forward.

Say you're a diary publisher like I was many years ago. There's nothing inherently unique about that. Debden, Daytimer, Collins, and Filofax all published day-books or organisers. All of them have daily pages, expense envelopes, and weekly planners. They all have $16 diaries and a range of up to a couple of hundred dollars. The unique element is what is conjured.

Our brand, NGT, started from humble beginnings, a family-owned business. We had the same products, a variation on a theme. So when the products are so similar, how do you then come up with something that separates you?

What could that be? Ease of purchase? A local office? Special treatment? Product knowledge? Faster? More helpful? I had to keep coming up with points of difference. And of course, none of them have YOU.

What we found in that business was that the features of the product were never as important as the delivery guarantee we gave with our products. Corporate customers could not afford to get their diaries and planners late each year.

The reality was that they were used to businesses that would send out to their best customers' products that usually were customised with their logo on the front cover and it was a reflection of their promise they had made to their customer.

We knew if we were to "guarantee delivery of their product

on time or their money back," it would stick as our industry was littered by corporates who were disappointed with a broken promises by a range of competitors.

Delivery of the Message

The last part of the theatre of the message to market is in the delivery of the message. You never want to appear that the answer is rehearsed and rote learned, even though in reality you have used the same message in every sales call.

The use of a pause, time to reflect while the question is being asked, all adds to the theatre and the suspense of the answer.

I always preface the answer with something like, 'If I had to think about it, a few things come to mind as to what separates us in the market…' and then I start to articulate a few key things.

You also don't have to "press play" when giving the answer, it doesn't need to be perfect.

So what happens if you are never asked that exact question, 'Why out of all the vendors available to me should I buy from you?'

That's okay, that's where real theatre come in. Simply ask the question of yourself in front of the buyer and then answer it. Just make sure you know the answer!

So it might go like this:

'You know, Jack, there is a question I get asked a fair bit whilst talking with people about our products and services. The question is why out of all the vendors available to me should I buy from your company? It's a great question… if I had to crystalise it in a few lines, I would say…'

Your buyer will be super impressed you know succinctly the answer to that question.

> ***Your message to market answers that number one question in sales: 'Out of all the options available to me, why should I buy from you?'***

This is worth rehearsing and getting it right. The application of this process is that it allows you to consistently tell the same story in your verbal presentations and also in your written word in proposals and copy. Write your answers on a pad, flesh them out, and keep it with you when you hit the road for a sales meeting. If you are a part of a larger sales team, spend some time brainstorming and using the collective wisdom of the team. Memorize those reasons before seeing buyers. Once you have got that clear in your mind, don't forget the most important person: the customer.

Your current customers will tell you some really important

things in answer to the question if you ask them. Sit back and listen, then go back to the office and re-work it. This is designed to be a dynamic process, one where there is no magic answer but what comes from trial and error. Then when you have it in draft form, go to the final stage.

We have pre-conceived ideas as to what the customer values, and when you think about it, the person who should be centre stage is the customer, so ask them!

Many years ago, when I started in the consulting business, I was designing my own message. I had a number of things down ready to discuss with the customer and see how they would register with them. I asked one of my clients if I could enlist their help.

I asked them for their feedback as to why they used my services? They replied to me, 'I really enjoy all of your material and I know the team gets a lot of benefit from it, but what I value more than anything else is my ability to get your opinion on things. You are my trusted advisor! I guess a sort of sounding board before I go ahead with any important sales decision.'

Trusted Advisor Selling was born off the back of that one conversation.

Great Theatre of the Sale Tip:

Of all the options available to customers why should they buy from me? List possible answers to that question. Come up with three key messages. Then develop backup evidence statements to support them and any collateral or demonstration that will back up your points. Lastly, rehearse it and put it to the test by asking your best customers why they use you. This will give you an important comparison to the message you designed.

Smart Questions

You may have heard the saying that "the better your question, the better the answer you'll get."

One benefit of asking great questions is that you learn a lot when listening to the reply.

I certainly believe that the better the question you ask, the better the impression you create in the buyer's mind and, logically, the more of a trusted advisor you can be.

Before listing five things that great questions achieve, I'd like to step back and look at questions as theatre. You've built the set, dressed for the part, defined the situation, told stories, used soundbites, and dramatised your unique point of difference. Questions can be used all through these procedures to enhance dramatic affect.

Questions are also testing points on the path to the confirmation of the sale. 'What do you think about what I've said?' is a typical "testing" question, but it's more than that. Its sub-script is, "Are you giving me your full attention?"

It is also a drama point. You go up-and-up-and-up with your presentation and suddenly you pass the ball:

'What do YOU think?' The buyer answers and so you build again—up-up-up (storytelling for example) and you stop again and ask another question. These questions draw the buyer into becoming an active participant in your dramatic monologue.

You might often pop in a question to which you already know the answer, a rhetorical question. (They're the best kind for retaining control.)

Such questions enable you to pause, wait for the buyer's answer, and without missing a beat (because you knew what they are about to say), confirm their answer with the word "right" and quickly move ahead. Proceed from there.

Here are **five good reasons** why to ask great questions.

1. *To gather information.* In other words, you're talking to learn.

2. *To create expert positioning*. Their answers help you frame up your message and position it to suit their needs.
3. *To influence and persuade*. The fact that you already know the answer doesn't mean you shouldn't ask the question. Their involvement in the question creates a pathway for the buyer to respond positively.
4. *To stimulate thought*. In other words, to get buyers thinking in areas they hadn't previously considered.
5. *To explore options*. To get the buyer to consider different options and different ways—that enables you to come up with a solution that is solely for them.

Expert questions in selling usually fall into one of **three types.**

1. ***Investigative questions.*** Here's an example. 'When I was on your website, I couldn't help but notice that you have [this]. Can you tell me more about it?' Investigative questions gets them talking—and who doesn't like to talk! It opens up the conversation and gives lots of air time.

2. ***Leading questions.*** An example might be, 'How important is it to your company that you benefit in this direction?' In other words, getting your buyer to contemplate the benefit of owning your product or solution.

3. ***A hypothetical question.*** 'How about we look ahead, say five years from now. Paint a picture for me of where you'd like to be in the marketplace?' In other words, hypothetically, what might happen?

Questions make you look intelligent; ask a great question and suddenly you are asked into the inner sanctum of the decision making.

You know when you have achieved this unique positioning as they trust you and may even ask you to keep the information discussed confidential.

Questions can also be too rote learned, too canned. I remember a bookkeeper coming in for an interview many years ago to ask me for the business and their first question was a very canned, 'So tell me what keeps you awake at night?' I thought for a moment and I then couldn't help myself, 'Nothing really, I sleep pretty well.' Not really kind of me, was it?

There was a massive assumption on their part that perhaps I was stressed and needed the help of a bookkeeper, but nothing was further from the truth.

I simply wanted a bookkeeper because I realised it was a poor use of my time and I could bill out my time at 10x the rate I was being charged by the bookkeeper.

When you have done your research and know about the company by guerrilla intelligence, you then can frame up a great opening question that can really knock the buyer over.

Make reference to their product range, their national coverage, years in business, their competitive advantage, website claims, etc., and then you are off and running!

When making a presentation in front of a management team or board of directors, do the work and find out who will be there and then frame up a question for each person based on what you are presenting, impressive!

If you are a member of a sales team, use a part of the sales meeting for role playing and creation of great questions. Throw down a challenge to each other to "plus" the idea by using better and better language.

I'm closing this chapter with a memory of an old-style sales trainer who used to teach that, when asking questions, his aim was to keep the buyer saying the word 'yes.'

'It's cold today?' Yes.

'Do you like this?' Yes.

'Do you like that?' Yes.

'Did you enjoy what I left you?' Yes.

Yes, yes, yes…

'Do you want to buy this product?'

Great Theatre of the Sale Tip:

Questions bring great insight to trusted advisors as long we listen for the reply! I don't prepare too many questions in advance. I want to be present. Take a moment before sales calls for research. Look at the company website. Look up your decision maker on LinkedIn. Reflect on what you've learned so that you can move the conversation forward.

Silence

I previously said one of the roles of a salesperson is to be an entertainer to get attention. Add to that: *another role of salesperson is to be an educator.*

The best way to get people to like you is to shut up and listen to what is important to them.

But selling is not a popularity quest. It's good to get liked at the start, but you're there to gain agreement and that isn't achieved by just talking and talking with the customer.

A salesperson does teach, but it must be seen in an advisory capacity where we are providing insight and a point of view they may not have considered.

A good friend of mine I mentioned previously, Jim Pancero, a trainer, mentor, and Hall of Fame Speaker with the National Speakers Association (USA), told me about coaching wannabe salespeople from a variety of companies many years ago as we watched them in the natural selling environment on the road.

He timed his students during sales calls they were making together with a stopwatch in his pocket while they went through their paces on the sales call. He concluded that 75 percent of the time they were doing the talking and less than 25 percent the buyer was verbalising their answers to the questions.

The point he made to me was that how can you as a salesperson really understand the needs and desires of the client if you are not listening to them but are jostling for airtime in the meeting? He also found that the nervous salesperson filled the space quickly when there was a period of silence instead of letting the pressure mount.

So what is the right percentage of time talking?

The right percentage might vary according to which style of buyer you have in front of you. A behavioural direct buyer will give short and sharp answers, generally, like talking in bullet points, whereas the interpersonal buyer who is much more heart focused or the cognitive detail focused one may naturally expand on their answers if they feel really comfortable. You see, you don't learn anything when you are doing the talking. It's in the active listening that you pick up not only what the buyer is saying, the way they are saying it, but also the nuances that happen in a sales call.

Just play the role and take the time you need to get your point across. Teaching leaves big opportunities for questions. You need that. You need give-and-take, parry-and-thrust. That speeds up the plot. And then, when you pause, there's silence.

Dramatic silence. Silence for effect.

I have always found that most people find silence uncomfortable in the sales meeting. Similar to doing sales consulting, mentoring, or holding a sales session with a number of salespeople. If I ask a question of a group and stand there long enough, someone will always rescue me with an answer or another question.

Silence builds the tension and creates the space for the buyer to ask another question or to let you know where they are in the decision making process.

When you ask a question of your buyer, hold that silent space without rushing to fill the gap. Then encourage a fulsome reply.

So why is listening so difficult for a great number of people in sales? Well, I think it usually comes down to a couple of key reasons. The first one is that the salesperson wants to make an impression or perhaps they really, really have to make this sale for the budget and the commission they need right now.

The second reason salespeople don't shut up and listen is because they are so excited about the product or solution that they are bursting with enthusiasm to show the customer the many benefits they can bring to the relationship.

The problem is that the buyer may for the first few minutes be excited that you are excited, but it doesn't take long for that to develop into boredom because they are secondary to the presentation of the salesperson and their ego.

There is power in silence; a pause will do wonders for your ability to control the conversation, it also makes you look more curious and more intelligent. If you find the concept hard to implement because you like to do so much of the talking, try counting to five and you should fix the problem.

Great Theatre of the Sale Tip:

Stop.

Let them fill the gaps.

Educators listen.

They pay attention.

It's all in character.

Powerful Analogies

I have mentioned two of the roles salespeople should play when selling.

The first is entertainer, to arouse the buyer's curiosity and capture attention. The second is the role of educator, which is about imparting information.

But that's not everything. You need other vehicles for transmitting facts, figures, and technical data.

Remember, people buy with their emotions and justify the purchase with logic. Stories alone are unlikely to carry the depth of information that tempts buyers to confirm their acceptance. You sometimes need to go a lot deeper to impart technical data.

You need to provide important information that allows buyers to "justify with logic" when they return to their desks. Buyers who do not comprehend the ins-and-outs of a proposition will not buy. Or if they do, they're the ones who return the product when they've gone back to their desks, thought it over, and felt the deal didn't stack up.

Sales people sometimes make the nuts and bolts of their product or service quite tricky to understand. Some customers commoditise the buying process and essentially don't care so much whom they buy from—they don't want to read the recipe; they just want the cake.

But most buyers take their purchases far more seriously. They may be highly qualified, which is how they got the job. Some have the relevant computer skills or an undergraduate degree relating to your product area. These people will want to understand the product's specifications concisely but in depth.

First, you must understand it yourself—if you can't, why are you here? Next, you have to tell the story cohesively from start to finish. Break the story up so you can fully explain the intricacies of why and when.

When salespeople enter a new industry, they have a need to get up to speed with great product knowledge.

I understand the need to understand the product and the solution, as you want to be able to talk with confidence about the product range. Whilst I totally agree product knowledge is key to success, there are usually about 80 percent of questions that are asked of 20 percent of the solutions you offer.

So you don't need to be a master of everything, just someone who can answer confidently the narrow band and then resource the other queries from other people in the organisation. I haven't met a buyer yet who won't let you come back to them quickly with the answer when you get back to the office—it goes to the heart of being the trusted advisor.

Great analogies come from knowing your product well and then finding creative ways of explaining it to your buyer so they get it.

There is no value in showing off to your buyer that you are a know-it-all (believe me I have met a number of these in sales) but rather someone who can involve the buyer by making it easily palatable.

Rehearse your knowledge to gain a full understanding first. I don't care how you do it, in front of the mirror, in front of your colleagues, or in your head, but do rehearse.

The weekly sales meeting is the most overlooked vehicle to brainstorm facts about your solution with each other, you will always learn something. And read. Read magazine articles that keep you abreast with the market in which you operate. That enables you to give a smart response if the customer says, 'Tell me something new.'

As you familiarise yourself with the wider implications of your product, let those thoughts roll around your head. They will generate ideas. Pick the best of them and compress their message into 20 word grabs.

Let those words lead your next thought-cycle and imagine you are explaining your product to a nine-year-old. I'm not kidding. Primetime television is pitched at nine-year-olds.

The President of the United States uses a vocabulary even a seven-year-old can understand. Simplicity sells. Make a difficult thing simple. A confused mind doesn't buy. It's the KISS principle and it works, at least for starters.

Do whatever it takes to make your story interesting and understandable in as few words as possible. Now it's time to transfer the knowledge, try an analogy. An analogy is a likeness between two or more things that form the basis of comparison. You can be more expansive, but here are two short ones:

'That's as useful as rearranging the deckchairs on the Titanic.'

Or,

'The universe is like a safe to which there is a combination, but the combination is locked up.'

Take all the time you need to come up with smart analogies. Build your case from there.

To create powerful analogies, ask:

- What is our product or service LIKE?
- Is there something you can compare that to?
- What's an interest your buyers generally have so can relate the product to that interest? For example football seems to always work: first quarter, last quarter, and one percenters are all things I have heard time and time again.
- Is your analogy something that your buyer will understand?

If you wanted to really customise the analogy, ask the buyer what their interests are and then when you find some common ground, use that common interest and then liken your product or service to that interest.

Pretend you're in front of the buyer and you're telling them about your product and service. '**You know, this product or service is just like…**' and then fill in the gap.

Analogies can come from sport, family, kids, world events, economy challenges, or a wide of other areas.

How do we deliver it in the theatre of the sale?

Here are some ways:

'I liken our XYZ product to...'

'Many clients have understood our solution by comparing it to...' 'When we designed our solution, we had ... in mind.'

One of the best analogies I ever heard was from a salesperson who was selling print management many years ago.

Their whole premise was that you don't have to buy the photocopier as they had them to rent and you just paid for the printing as you went along.

We were in front of the buyer and they asked them about the fleet of the cars they had for the sales people parked in the front of reception that we noticed on the way in. They simply made reference to it and drummed home their point.

'I couldn't help notice as we made our way into the front door today the fleet of cars you had there in the front for the salespeople and service technicians. How often do you update them? Do you own them outright or do you lease them?'

The answer was of course that the company updated them about every five years and they are on hire purchase agreements, and he knew it.

He simply said to the buyer, 'Just like your cars out front, we offer the same leasing service. We update the photocopiers at all your branches every –three to five years and all you pay is the usage per click for the printing. Why pay for the machine when you don't need to? They only depreciate in value and you then have to go to market and sell them.'

Great Theatre of the Sale Tip:

Your analogy doesn't have to be complicated. You may know your product backwards, but can your customer understand it? They may not tell you as they don't want to seem like a dill, so jump in and use an analogy to cut through your message. Try one and then brainstorm it with members of your team or in the office.

Words That Sell & Words That Don't

If you want to position yourself as a true trusted advisor and an authority with what you know, your language in a meeting is critical. Consider the speak of the industry (**table turns** or covers in the restaurant business, or the number of **SKUs** in the office products industry, or perhaps **balloon payments** or trade values in the car, truck, and ag sales businesses). Learn the words, the shorthand version.

Learn new words, spend some time with Roget's Thesaurus and learn words you don't know. The wider the vocab, the better the positioning you will create in the meeting. This is especially important when you are selling up in the C-Suite.

American sales trainer Tom Hopkins talks about rejection words. Some of those might be listed in the first column below. I like to also talk about those words that make the buyer salivate as per the right-hand column words.

I ask: 'In the language of the sale, what words attract?'

Try these:

Salesperson Words	Trusted Advisor Words
Cost	**Investment**
Contract	**Paperwork or Agreement**
Deal	**Partnering**
Quote	**Proposal**
Pitch	**Presentation**
Approve	**Authorise**
Buy	**Own**

The first column is old-talk, the second column is trusted advisor talk. Convert your language from the left-hand column to the right-hand column.

No one wants to buy something that costs them money, but

they are much more attracted to it if they think it will make them money or save them money, then it becomes an investment. When you talk about "giving someone a quote," you are now sounding like the tradie who wants to paint your fence or to repair your appliance, but when you change the language to "a proposal," it has much more weight in a white collar business-to-business meeting. You have thought about their needs and you have put together a recommendation of the way forward for them, that's the inference.

> ***A hallmark of effective presenters is their ability to express the desired message in as few* words *as possible.***

Economy of words is a big plus. Get the right words, keep it tight, then tell 'em and tell 'em and tell 'em. And when they've "got it," use influential words to encourage them to take the next step.

I favour words like:

- easy
- new
- guarantee
- proven
- save
- results

Knowing that one of the core drivers of buyers is to have their life made easy, bringing "easy" into the conversation has always developed rapport for me. The right words need to be deliberate and used on the back of what you are hearing from the buyer. Get used to slipping them into your sentences. And, like I've said all through this book, rehearse your script until you "own" the words.

These words are "warming" words, they provide safety (guarantee) or are the latest in the market (new) or perhaps there is significant evidence about their success rate (proven). The great thing about proven and guaranteed as words is that it creates a lead in to a conversation about how you do it, how you back it up.

Repeating the Words that Your Buyer Uses

I wish I had a dollar for each time a salesperson missed the point that the buyer was making whilst I have accompanied them on a coaching call out in the field. **What** the buyer is saying to you is critical, but just as critical is the **way** they are saying it to you as well.

In the meeting, consider: Repeating back to the buyer the last few words of the sentence they have just finished. Consider key words they keep repeating, it leads you to the drivers of the buyer.

Listen for how they describe things.

If my buyer says to me 'there needs to be a good return on investment' at the end of a point they are making when talking about sales training, I will then lead with, 'We expect our sales training to provide at least a 10x return on any investment you make in my services.' This is not a big claim given that if they have a sales team of 8-10 in the field, it might only represent a couple of extra sales each.

In the written form, I always listen for how a buyer describes the type of products or services that I offer.

I had a buyer recently say to me, 'I need a back-to-basics sales program for my national sales team.' So… hey, presto, in my proposal, my program was no longer described in the recommendations as the Trusted Advisor Selling Program but was now the "Back to Basics Foundational Selling Program."

Your buyer's language is critical to the way they communicate, and when you can start to use their vernacular, it makes you a trusted advisor in their industry and not someone who is selling a solution with no industry experience. The funny thing is that you don't even have to fully understand what exactly some of that language means, just the overall intent and the meaning.

I remember seeing a new prospect for our diary and organiser range when I started in sales some 30 plus years ago. They were in the real estate industry and were talking about "listings" and I had no idea what they meant. One thing I quickly realised was that these listings were important and he was really upset that the sales team was down the previous year and that this would have a real impact on them making their income targets.

I kept repeating back to him that 'listings were critical and the diary organiser he was looking at would be very valuable to him and his team in keeping track of how they were spending their time and would produce more listings by following up on prospects and proposals they had presented.' He agreed and then bought the time management systems for his team.

I was automatically an expert who really had no idea what he was talking about. That's the power of great language and the talk of the buyer.

Great Theatre of the Sale Tip:

Clarify your message. Punctuate the message with words to insert into the dialogue. Use the thesaurus to add new ones regularly. Be a student of language. Notice the difference it makes, how many more buyers become engaged and salivate when you talk with them. Make the words yours.

Pitch to Your Buyer's Style & Preferred Mode of Receiving Communication

When I attended one of my first sales training courses in the 1980s, our trainer taught us that when it comes to preferred means of receiving communication, people fall into three types. The categories are visual, auditory, and kinaesthetic (touch). Most people prefer a combination of all three, favouring one predominant form of communication.

That's handy to know.

It's all to do with their upbringing, cultural cues, and sociology. An example of a cultural cue is kinaesthetic communication. Mediterranean cultures tend to touch more than northern Europeans and so do older folk, like US politician Joe Biden and actor Dustin Hoffman until younger people complained and a whole movement was born.

I'm the visual type. I have to see that PowerPoint presentation right in the front of my eyes. The pictures and the graphs do it for me.

Conversely, they say one picture is worth 1,000 words, but that's not true for people who make decisions on the basis of what they hear. You can pick out these people because when you phone them, they don't require anything else but your voice in order to say yes to the proposition.

What this means is that once you've worked out within which category your buyer fits, you can talk directly to that aspect of their behavioural style and win. You'll get a lot of clues from their choice of words.

Visual buyers will favour seeing-words like envisage, focus, and looking. Auditory buyers might favour something like, 'That resonates with me,' or 'That sounds interesting.' "Resonates" and "sounds" are clues that you can trade on.

Kinaesthetic buyers talk in terms of how something feels to them. They might also be addressing the potential team response to the question.

From the prospect's choice of language to using your own intuition, figure out which of the three you should perform to in your next sales call and deliver accordingly. Prepare to that aspect of the prospect's personality.

Visual: If it's a visual person, bring visual aids. Visual customers are unlikely to forgive you if you don't know how to use PowerPoint or didn't bring the maps.

Auditory: Auditory types might care less about those visuals because they want you to talk them into the purchase. With them, think about tone and speed of speech.

Kinaesthetic: When dealing with kinaesthetic types, place the item in their hands. Once they're holding it, hopefully they won't hand it back.

> ***This threefold division of the type of audience you're playing to is useful because it gives you three slightly different approaches to rehearse.***

If you know your sales presentation three different ways, I'd say you're in pretty good shape.

Aside from the V-A-K distinction we make, great salespeople have done a good deal of work on behavioural styles. While there are plenty of models to choose from—with a choice of types of birds or animals or just descriptors around a variety of models—I am amazed how many salespeople I have trained who don't seem to have much knowledge of them.

Perhaps I am too close to it and used to working with these styles all the time?

Study the DISC, Myers Briggs, or, the one I prefer, the CRG Sales Style Indicator model from Canada and you will gain an appreciation of the style of the person in front of you. This will give you an enormous advantage in the market and instant rapport if you can be sharp enough to pick up on the style and then talk the right language.

The four styles CRG has studied and written comprehensively about are the following:

Behavioural style (direct and assertive)

Cognitive style (detail oriented and technical)

Interpersonal (heart and team player)

Expressive (talkative and extroverted)

I have summarised them just because there is such a body of work around these styles and my purpose here is to get on with the transfer value in terms of the theatre of the sale. I am a certified partner with the organisation and use their profiles when I do sales recruitment for some of my clients. To really acknowledge and uncover the full style profile, you need to look at three dimensions to style:

* extroversion / introversion

* people / facts

* verbal / non-verbal

We are, of course, made up of all these dimensions and we are talking about your preference.

People also may have a style bias, but they can be quite different in a buying mode compared with how they might be at the pub on a Friday night with friends.

To be able to see the cluster of actions, verbal response, and the nature of the buyer unfold in front of you, you then make a call (be careful!) that the person you are talking with has a predominance of X style. The reason why I say be careful is that we know that people are indeed made of all four styles and will not always be consistent in the way they appear in terms of style.

With that in mind, you can now be a little more targeted in your communication and see what rapport you develop. For example, someone who is feeding back to you a lot of technical questions gives out a hint that they are cognitive by nature. If it is coupled with a strong opinion, they may also have a high degree of behavioural in their style as well. The exciting thing about the person in front of you is that if you can provide a compelling argument of facts, they may be very impressed and talk themselves into the sale.

Similarly, someone who is expressive and outgoing by style is someone who will want to talk a great deal about anything. I have found them to be loose on time generally (making massive assumptions here!), and so you need to make sure in between all the conversation, which is 80 percent their way, that you just punctuate the talk with some direction!

The key here is awareness and being present or you will miss it, or worst yet, you will jump to conclusions which can be dangerous! We are looking for clusters, and not just a one-off attribute of the buyer, that will help us to determine how we should engage them. Are you watching out for the signals from your buyer's behaviour? Are you trying to listen to not just the words they are using but where they place emphasis on the words and the actions that go with the words?

I think customers and prospects leave clues to salespeople in sales presentations, once you take the pressure off yourself and your "stuff" and be totally present and watch for the nuances, life changes. There is a flipside to this. We have talked about the buyer, their style preference and preferred mode of communication, how about your bias? This can have an impact on your level of theatre and which of these 25 ideas you feel more comfortable implementing.

Become a good student of your style and your way of communicating.

Ask yourself whether your style will blend well with the customer in front of you. It's interesting to consider it as I have worked with many sales managers over time where they have had to make decisions to move salespeople off accounts and re-assign a different salesperson to that customer because they clashed with the buyer. How obvious are your preferences? Do you talk a lot in the meeting generally? Are you fairly assertive in your presentation? Do you get caught up in detail when you start to talk about the facts and figures related to the product?

How about the facts bias versus a people bias?

If you have an interpersonal style buyer in front of you, can you move quickly from facts into heart statements and observations? If you can crack the code on this, it really does make a big difference to your ability to get into rapport and then to convert the business. The moment I studied style and peoples' communication preference, my selling changed and I turned the spotlight much more on the buyer and off me as the seller. This lead to much more targeted communication where I believe I made many more sales.

Great Theatre of the Sale Tip:

Study style communication preferences. It's worth the effort and it will give you so much intelligence when talking with your buyer. When you know them and their preferences, you can then tailor your message by thinking about pace, tonality, and what character you may need to play in the theatre.

Put the Elephant in the Room

Author Mark Twain said the advantage of always telling the truth is you don't have to remember anything.

One of the best ways to develop rapport with buyers is to be absolutely honest and transparent with the customer always.

The greatest acting teacher of the 20th century, Constantin Stanislavsky, developed what came to be famously known as "Method Acting." This is the man who taught Marlon Brando, Al Pacino, Marilyn Monroe, Dennis Hopper and Robert De Niro. He taught that real truth is predicated on the actors not being aware of the imaginary nature of their performance. He's saying that actors have to believe in their performance, they must not "act."

If you're faking, you don't really believe.

In order to believe in your sales performance, you have to believe in your product, so it follows that you transmit your belief.

By being transparent when someone else's product or solution is better suited to a certain industry segment and you have a specialty in a different segment, it may work for you to call this out. I am not saying for a moment that you want to give away every opportunity to your competitor, but remember, not every buyer is going to buy from you no matter how good you are!

So… letting the buyer know that your company has a number of clients you serve that just so happen to be a part of their industry while your competitors focus on something different will add weight to your argument if you know they are not going to proceed with your proposal.

I have found in my sales career that sometimes you're just not a good fit for the potential customer in front of you; it might be a style clash, values misalignment or a philosophy on buying cheap rather than a quality, premium solution. It's especially important in selling services as you are going to have to work with that person and you don't want it to be a grind each day.

It could also be the price conversation where you cannot lie about a cheaper solution when asked. However, that's only where it starts and not where it ends. Putting the elephant in the room upfront unloads everything that might be seen as fake about your performance. It creates trust because there's an admission of transparency. No lies. The tricky part is gone. It creates an aura of credibility almost instantaneously. Being blatantly open allows you to relax into your selling role.

Some years ago, I was accompanying a sales person on a call in the agricultural industry; tractors, sprayers, and combine harvesters were his product on offer. We called on Harley—that was the farmer's name. And Harley said to the salesperson with great theatre, 'I've had your competitor come and see me and I got a quote for that new tractor and you are 15-20 percent more expensive than your competitor' (a considerable percentage in a market where you can run up a bill of some hundreds of thousands of dollars for a new tractor).

Then there was silence.

It was one of my first sales calls accompanying any salesperson in agricultural sales back then and I wasn't sure what to expect. Watching Harley give this objection, I was interested in how the salesperson might react. Without missing a beat, the salesperson fired back, 'That surprises me Harley, I would have expected us to be at least 25-30 percent more.' I really didn't expect him to say that. He went on, 'Our product is the best on the market. We offer a more comprehensive service and backup over the course of a lifetime. When your lights are on, our lights are on. So that price difference really doesn't add up to much when you're keeping the tractor for 15 years or so.'

Checkmate!

I think the thing that made the answer so effective was that he didn't flinch with Harley when he delivered it and looked him square in the eye!

That's a great example of putting the elephant in the room because it handles the difficult price objection upfront. The salesperson unloads which makes him/her totally comfortable with the role. It's also a great understanding of the theatre of the sale.

By the way, Harley bought.

The Volkswagen car puts the elephant in the room all the time in their marketing. When VW was trying to break into the American market in the 1950s, it carried a lot of baggage, not the least that it was a German car in the afterglow of the Second World War.

Also, it was nothing like American cars of the same period. American cars were getting bigger and more powerful, that was what customers apparently wanted. So the VW ad campaign ran a headline, "Think Small," which turned the so-called disadvantage into a positive upfront statement.

Another VW campaign did the same thing in a different way. It read, "Our engine has no Super-Turbo injector," an argument for mind over eye, flattering the customer with the inference that s/he was smart enough to appreciate the invisible technical changes rather than the superficial exterior.

How about the earlier Avis campaigns in car rental? Knowing they were number two behind Hertz in the market with a long way to make up gave Avis a great opportunity to not hide the fact but actually to make a point of it. Their campaigns focused on the fact that their lines were always shorter than Hertz, so why wait, come and see us. They were also very clever in taking a "we try harder" position in their advertising.

Another way of being upfront is totally admitting when you've made a blunder.

Diffuse any situation by unequivocally stating you are wrong. It's amazing how forgiving buyers can be when dealing with openness. 'Sorry, I was wrong' is pretty disarming.

One of the years in the diary business we had a challenging time in getting our product in from overseas and a number of deliveries ran late with our customers in NZ. It wasn't actually our fault as the manufacturer made promises they couldn't keep, but really that didn't matter as the buyer had a contract with us and not them!

So spending time talking about their inability to get the product out the warehouse door was counterproductive as the buyer would only think that the same thing could happen the next year, and with an 85 percent retention rate all of our corporate accounts held, that wasn't smart business.

The next year rolls around and now we had to approach all of those NZ customers again to secure the forward order. You can imagine the angst in going back to those customers you had let down hoping to get their business in the following year! My newly appointed NZ sales manager said he would approach all the customers and ask for their forgiveness as this was his territory. It's certainly easier to approach a customer when you are the salesperson on the account and you were not with the company the previous year.

Graham was an experienced salesperson, a man who firmly believed in the theatre of the sale—when he approached each customer, he turned around, poked his backside out to them, and asked them to have a "kick" as we had let them down. He then turned to them and said to them, 'But we won't let you down this year!'

Dale Carnegie mentions in his book *How to Win Friends and Influence People* that when you are wrong, admit it emphatically! Assess the situation, just become the person you really are, and when the problem-situation has settled, list the advantages of your product and its disadvantages.

It's person-to-person now. No one is faking anything. This is the first step on the path to trusted advisor selling.

Buyers like honesty and transparency and it is the currency for developing trust for the trusted advisor. My theory is that you may as well get to them before they get to you; in other words, they will find out, it's only a matter of time, and that won't be good when they do!

Put the elephant in the room at the outset, and because you did that, you'll find yourself comfortably performing within an honest space. It can also be a proactive way to jump on the offensive and to build a case in advance of the meeting so you are aware of your facts.

Where do you need to go on the offensive?

Great Theatre of the Sale Tip:

When you know you are wrong, admit it. It will bring you brownie points for sure. When you know you have a solution that is not as attractive on price, circumvent the conversation by letting them know that you would not expect to be the cheapest, 'However, these are things you get with our solution that no one else is offering.'

Speed is Your Competitive Advantage & It Makes Great Theatre

Speed is your competitive advantage in the new crazy busy marketplace.

When I began selling, we were sped up by the fax machines and later came mobile phones the size of small bricks. Before that, it was even slower. Someone would ask for a quote and we'd send the quote back via snail mail.

Expectations are much faster now. Within the hour is good. Buyers want immediacy. If I don't get back to prospects within the hour, I am giving up a massive competitive advantage. If I don't respond quickly to a service enquiry, I don't want them to feel afraid they'll be sent back to square one and will have to start over from the scratch.

They have made a decision in our favour, to either ask for a quote or hopefully buy. They believed in the credibility of your performance and quick response is part of that. Don't let them down now. Buyers don't want a long-winded response. They don't expect you to write an essay. They're not looking for a perfectly written email. They're looking for a speedy acknowledgement. Sometimes a short, one-line response is enough to keep buyers happy. Acknowledging their question might be all that's required on your part. 'Thanks, I'll get back to you real soon,' 'Appreciate it,' or, 'I'll have that answer to you in an hour' might be all you need to keep them warm.

In its most basic form, think for a moment of how you feel when you are not acknowledged in a retail shop. This shop does not deserve my business I can hear you saying. And yet, we put up with it, because it has become the norm and not the exception.

When you respond quickly, either to a new quote or an existing client, whether it be sales related or something more like an after-service enquiry, you create a perception in the mind of the customer. This person values my business, they care for my business, they do what they say they will!

Here are some ways to create a healthy perception in the mind of the buyer that you treat speed as a competitive advantage:

- You get back to people quickly between each meeting and also between the meeting and the promised proposal (24-48 hours shows intent).
- You find a reason to get back to them in between meetings with a question of clarification if you are not able to see them to keep the opportunity alive (due to their end not yours) for at least a week or so.
- You re-confirm all meetings in advance to make sure you don't have that cancelled meeting or the buyer doesn't show up!
- You send back a short action plan from the meeting with joint accountabilities spelt out so you can continue to move forward.
- You understand that the theatre of the sale is not a 9 to 5 job. When the buyer is ready to receive your proposal or the follow-up call, you do whatever it takes to get back to them, even if that means 6 p.m. on phone or later on email.

Speed is great theatre, with the general level of responsiveness overall in the market as very average,

You will stand out immediately to the buyer when you are on the other end of the phone or email responding to their enquiry within 10 minutes.

Text messages and people using iPads on the move has meant that we forgive now the beautifully laid out letter format. Even a text with a thumbs up can be taken as communication currency that works in some quarters and is a great example of the "speed of acknowledgement" principle.

When you consider the amount of time and effort sometimes to gain commitment from your buyer to go and see them, to listen, and then present some ideas, I don't understand why you wouldn't want to make sure that they think of you favourably after the meeting.

We are mobile sales teams now serving the needs of our customers and being at their service for enquiries, so there really isn't any excuse. After all this effort to prepare a performance and stage it, it seems silly to put the brakes on now. Adopt the philosophy of "under promise and over deliver," think about what you promise in terms of turnaround times.

On just about every occasion I can think of, the timeframe I promised was a good deal faster than what the buyer was expecting.

Even if I know I can get the proposal back to them that night, I will quote them the next day and then beat the timeframe and actually get it to them at night if required on email and I cannot get to them face to face.

Build a reputation for being ultra-responsive and you become more referable; people know that you will not only deal with the referred lead in a respectful manner but you will also ooze timeliness.

Great Theatre of the Sale Tip:

Everything matters, especially your keenness to get back to the customer and show your appreciation for their business and for the opportunity to provide your ideas and solutions. Remember that their time is one of the most precious commodities they have; don't play with it or you will create a poor piece of theatre.

Remind Your Buyer of Your Value

Once you have left the customers premises your future role in the relationship can be solidified by taking an action which is proactive.

As trusted advisors, we are in the business of adding value. And "adding value" is empirical, meaning your success can be measured in numbers.

The theatre of selling runs like this: when someone enters the presence of others, they seek information about that person. Information is shown two ways.

Firstly by sign-vehicles (as applied to their stereotype), for example, the Rolex watch or a $10 watch are both sign vehicles.

Secondly, we glean clues from (1) the salesperson's conduct and (2) whatever backgrounding or experience we may have had with his/her company. We accept the rest on faith, hoping the interaction will be mutually profitable.

When advisors make recommendations that lead to measurable improvements, that's much more than a sign-vehicle. It's confirmation that the advisors are everything they said they are. They can therefore be trusted. Remember the old sales adage: "it's six times easier to sell more to an established client than to go out and get a new one"? (By the way, I think it's more like 10-20 times.)

So why wouldn't you want to make sure that the customer sees the value in what you do and that it would take a really good reason to change.

Reminding your customer of your value is a clever way of preserving the relationship.

It also makes sure you are planting the seed ahead of the next negotiation or bidding process. It stops them in their tracks when they get that telemarketing call or short email from another provider with the much cheaper lead in price. It doesn't have to be all about you bragging about how good you are, it can be as simple as you making sure that they are happy with the way you handled something. It's up to you to leverage your credibility, which will never be higher than the moment you confirm and deliver on the sale.

Here are two examples of where we can prepare in advance so as to remind the customer of the value to our client relationship, using theatre to cement the relationship.

The first situation arises before we arrive at the client's premises when we are visiting someone for a repeat visit.

We should get a clear idea of how to move clients closer to their personal and professional goals. To do that, you must understand what their goals are, from which you'll deduce how you can add value. Read the signs. Study up on their previous orders, quotes, buying patterns, and also check with customer service to make sure there is nothing you don't know about the back end fulfilment of their orders.

Knowing that they have no service issues, that the goods have been delivered on time and that the account is all paid up on time is important information in being able to have a conversation around "are you happy with our performance?"

The second situation is to not leave a client's premises without reminding them of the value you have just created. Salespeople undervalue their expertise. They begin and end with a conversation about product. Create a loop instead. Be clear on how you have added value and remind the client of what you have achieved together. This is how you create an ongoing loop in your relationship.

Perhaps something as simple as asking the customer, 'Are you happy with the savings we achieved in comparison to what you were looking for that we first spoke about?' (when you already know they are!). Alternately, you may leave the meeting with a short verbal summary as to where you are with a project and show you are meeting the desired outcomes. This is all proof, evidence that they have made the right choice. It also helps when they go to update the boss and can recite your language in support of the results you are achieving.

Another way of making sure we cement the value in the buyer's mind is to ask them if there is anything else you can do for them. Not asking with hooks where you are trying to write another order. I am talking about anything they might need (a quiet word to customer service, checking on an order in the warehouse, etc.) and then make sure you do it!

Reminding the customer of the value of what you are doing for them is also the perfect lead in to asking for the referral. As my good friend Bill Cates (The Referral Coach) says, 'The best time to ask for a referral is when value has been acknowledged.'

And it gets easier

and easier

and easier

with each subsequent performance.

Great Theatre of the Sale Tip:

Retaining clients is all about going the extra mile and pre-empting issues in advance so nothing comes as a surprise. It's all about the proactive mind-set of selling, and reminding them of the value of your relationship is a key piece of creating great engagement and theatre.

Take Notes & the Old-Fashioned Thank You Note!

Does it bug you when you go out for dinner with your spouse or loved one and you are asked for your order by the waiter or waitress and when you give your preferences but they make no notes whatsoever?

I am sure it's meant to impress me that they can remember all the details and not have to write them down, but to be honest, it just cheeses me off.

I want them to get it right and my expectation is that they don't have to remember the order, just to write it down!

The same applies to sales and getting down all the details of a business-to-business sales meeting with a buyer. But the theatre of the sale dictates that it represents more than this.

My dad always taught me that in each sales meeting you always make notes! He was the first mentor I ever took advice from in sales and it proved to be gold.

It's important you get down relevant information but it's more important the process of writing that will be attractive to the buyer.

Dad's theory was that if you are making notes as the buyer is talking, automatically they think that what they are telling you is really important to the solution and the process of collecting valuable intelligence.

We are saying subliminally to the customer or prospect that I am here for you, I am wanting to understand you. I am wanting to deliver the very best solution to you.

The real story is that it may not be the case. The reality is that most things we learn from a sales meeting with a prospect or customer we have heard before.

Certain products or solutions they are seeking, problems they have had before, and price points they are trying to reach. I don't mean to be cruel or disrespectful, it's just the truth.

Most people have similar problems or concerns and they

want similar solutions.

And… this is where the theatre comes to the fore.

Playing our role, we are there to listen, so listen.

We are there to learn, so learn.

The Other Reason

I always think it's prudent not to rely on your memory as well. Nothing worse than coming back to the office and trying to remember exactly what you said you would quote on.

As a buyer, I used to always hate it when the sales person on the next visit would say, 'I think I got this right' or, 'I was going to ask you for clarity on…' or a phone call in between meetings where I have to repeat myself again.

If you are a professional, you will have what you need before you leave the sales call and should be able to put together a proposal that meets those objectives and outcomes. Don't rely on memory if you tend to forget things.

Making notes at the meeting also gives you a great opportunity to note the language the customer uses.

This can form the basis of the "situation summary" or the objectives of the proposal if you are providing services.

It might also give you really important lingo of the industry, and when you can recite these back in the next meeting, it's really impressive.

Making notes in combination with nodding at the customer is about creating a deeper connection; look them in the eyes and repeat back what they just said.

Then ask if it's okay to make a note of that. Now you have really got the triple. (By the way, I have never in 35 years of selling ever had someone say that they didn't want me to make notes!)

The challenge of the sales call with the "triple"—looking at them, nodding, and making notes—means that you may find it hard to decipher your notes later.

There have been many times I have left the appointment and then gone back to the office only to think to myself "what the heck have I written down, I can't read it!"

But you are looking for a single word or a phrase to trigger, and that's what is important to write down.

Get the key facts down but never—and I repeat, never—turn up to a meeting without a notebook and knowledge of your diary and meetings you have planned over the next week.

The Old-Fashioned Thank You Note ...

Call me old fashioned, but when was the last time you received a handwritten note or a card thanking you for the business?

Never?

I am not sure where that simple technique ever went. I guess we got digital; we just email them now.

Yes, I can understand the expediency value to you of doing that. But… that's the whole reason why a handwritten thank you note makes a really great impression.

It says "I am happy to go the extra mile and I also want to stand out."

Just think about it, there are so many opportunities to thank the prospect or customer:

Thank you for the meeting and your time.

Thank you for the opportunity to put together a proposal.

Thank you for the order.

Thank you for the ongoing business.

Thank you for your attendance at a function.

Thank you for the referral or introduction.

You get the idea…

Just thank them, because no one ever does it!

As a piece of theatre, I think there is enormous value to receive something that is handwritten—it says quality, it says "I am willing to spend a buck or two on you," it says "you are important."

I have a system that had worked for me for many years and it helps to develop rapport and likeability.

After my first appointment with a potential customer, I will go to my car where I have a box in the boot with blank printed thank you cards.

I will take one out and write a handwritten message to thank them for their time and for asking me to put together a proposal. Then I'll drop it into an express post bag that I also have in the boot and include a copy of one of my books with a handwritten note. I then drop by one of the yellow express post boxes on my way home. They should receive the parcel within the next 24 hours.

It buys me time in between meetings and makes sure the buyer has me at the front of their mind. It then provides a nice link at the start of the next meeting when the buyer will invariably say thank you for the book.

I have a real estate agent who sold an investment property for me many years ago in North Melbourne and he had a system of hand signed letters and cards—the month after sale, year after sale, and then every year after.

I have kept them all through the years as I use them in class to show a committed salesperson example and how they have invested in the relationship. I am up to his seventh year card, that's impressive!

I guess you could say the same for the emailed Christmas card or the emailed birthday card; they just don't do it for me. I won't remember you if you send one because I got a heap of them every year, but the person who sends me a note in the mail, they stand out!

Great Theatre of the Sale Tip:

Thank your clients. It doesn't take much really. Get some cards printed at the local Officeworks, pop your logo and/or face on them, and don't print anything on the inside. Now as you find the occasion, simply take one, make a note, and drop it in the mailbox. It's that easy. Yes, it costs you a little more but what is a client relationship worth?

Be the Magnet - Be Easy to Deal With!

I really believe that people buy from people they like and trust and who are easy to deal with.

The question is, what can you do to be more likeable? Can you create theatre to be easy to deal with? I think the best theatre comes from the prepared spontaneity, when you have choreographed the performance but never look like you are in the theatre of the sale.

It can be a little rehearsed; in fact, I think there is real value in planning your entry to the meeting—what you will say, how you can have a little energy about you.

Buyers will be much more attracted to us and our presentation when we:

1. **Smile.** It's amazing how your whole face lights up with a smile and how warm it makes the conversation with a buyer.

2. **Are positive about our business, their business, and the market.** People like positive people. There is nothing worse that the sour puss salesperson who looks like the world is falling apart.

3. **Don't get caught up in the gossip of business.** Some people love gossip—who is moving to where, competitors' challenges, etc. It is not professional and it looks ugly.

   Say 'Yes, I can do that.' Optus created a whole campaign around the "yes" in business; sure beats looking like it's all too difficult.

4. **Take a genuine interest in the buyer**—their interests, holidays, challenges. Genuine is the key word, you actually want to know what has been happening with their company and how they are doing personally.

   Acknowledge an incoming email or call urgently. As mentioned in the last chapter, speed provides you with a true competitive advantage in the market.

Do something the client didn't expect. Add some value, give extra personal service to make sure the order or process goes smoothly.

5. **Use strong non-verbals.** Nod when the prospect makes an interesting point or is passionate about their point of view.

Client Buying Signals

I was tempted to write a whole chapter just on this one idea, but the idea is so simple that it didn't require it. But… it's so powerful. In essence, salespeople today are not always watching for the signals at every meeting.

> ***Remember, the experienced buyer is also in character most of the time playing their role.***

The way they react to a price, a value proposition, or a recommendation can be well and truly rehearsed. There are always two conversations going on in any sales presentation. The first conversation is the information exchange. The second conversation is what you observe in their behaviour.

Buying signals we need to look out for are either verbal or non-verbal.

When we talk about **verbal** buying signals, we look for things that the buyer says that takes us into the future. They may mention that there is a timeframe connected with moving ahead, needing a certain colour or style, asking about payment terms, or perhaps even breaking down the quantities for delivery.

In discussing my consulting services with a potential customer, I always look for when they want to involve someone else's opinion on the sales call. They might go into the business owner's office and ask them to join us and introduce me and my Trusted Advisor Selling Method. This is a very good sign.

In terms of **non–verbal** behaviour I have observed, here are the ones that I think we should be watching out for:

1. The client leans forward when I am making a point.

I watch body language in the selling process and look for what the buyer is telling me. If they change their state physiology and lean into the proposal or the outline of the solutions I am presenting, I am excited about the possibilities. They may also ask if we can move to the meeting table instead of their desk, which now gives me a great opportunity to take advantage of things like the flipchart and whiteboard.

2. **A smile and positive acknowledgment I am getting from the buyer.**

A smile tells you a lot in presenting, whether that be the one-to-one conversation or a one-to-many conversation while on the platform. I have always thought the person in front of me is saying, "I am in sync with you, what you are saying is making a heck of a lot of sense!"

3. **They are studying my materials, collateral, or order forms.**

There is something about touch and the engagement it creates. A prospect may show little sign of being in buying mode up until that point and then things change immediately when they start to look over materials, handouts with my training sessions, and coaching products. When they then ask if they can keep it and start to doodle all over the sheet of paper with asterisks and dollar signs, I know something is shifting inside of them.

4. **Taking out a calculator and looking at various numbers.**

Calculations on a calculator or long-hand arithmetic on a notepad is saying to me, "I want to see if I can make this work! Let's see if I can get this through." They may also get to a conclusion straight away that it's not going to be easy.

5. Repeated nodding to the points I make in the meeting.

Like the smile from a one-to-one meeting or on the platform, I love to see nodding to the points I am making. Again, it shows me we are on the same page. "I like what you have to say, you are making sense to me!"

6. Looking quizzically to gain more clarity

"I am curious but I need a little more understanding! Not sure that what you are saying is sitting well with me, I am feeling a little incongruence in the message."

I used to deal with a manufacturer in China many years ago and he was the king at this last move.

He would seem to take an eternity to re-work a target price I had given him and then shake his head as if it couldn't possibly be done.

He would then ring down to the floor of the factory and speak in Chinese with an assertive tongue to influence those down there to come up with the answer he was looking for in terms of savings they could muster to reach my target price.

I always knew it was a game he was playing and he always got to the price I was after; it was just so much fun watching him work his magic!

A magnetic personality starts with the entry to reception and announcing that you are there for the meeting.

The small talk you make and taking an interest in their life and how long they have been in the company goes a long way to the theatre coming to life. It then extends to the buyer when they join you, but it also includes to an introduction of anyone else in the business. You never know who else may be in the final decision making if you haven't found this out in advance!

A magnetic personality is then visible in the way that you answer the phone; you are always on show. People don't want to know that you are having a bad day or that you haven't had your lunch yet or that your relationship with the warehouse might be needing a mediator!

Great Theatre of the Sale Tip:

Magnetism, or likeability as I call it in my workshops, can be consciously created. It's about the first phone call, the re-confirmation of an appointment; the moment of truth and first impression you create when you walk through the door the first time you meet the buyer. Everything matters.

Third Party Social Proof

Have you noticed the way people will trust what others are saying about you more than what you say about yourself?

This is the secret of the third party endorsement for the work that we do!

This is theatre at its finest, creating an influencing moment and someone else provides the evidence for you! A very happy customer who has been a client for many years and a discussion about how the solution has worked for them is a big plus.

How the team loves your product, how you personally are a trusted advisor to their business, is all going to do the heavy lifting in your sales process.

There are levels of social proof in the theatre of the sale.

At the bottom of the ladder is simply a **like or comment** made to a posting or article or video you have popped up in LinkedIn. Good, but not earth shattering. The next level is the **testimonial in writing** by the client which you can post up on your LinkedIn profile page and use in various printed forms, such as collateral. This can be transferred to the website, a sales page, or capability statement. By the way, in order to make your customers' lives easy, I have also found that so many of my raving fans have been really keen for me to write my own testimonial. They are just too busy and if I leave them tasked with doing it, I may never get it. So I provide suggested language.

The second highest level is the **client who is prepared to go on video for you.** It can be as simple as just a few words on an iPhone, and hey, presto, it's up on the website, social media posts, or a link in the email proposal they can watch. No longer do you have to go to a studio and to set up lights, cameras, action with your customer to record a testimonial. You simply pull out your mobile phone and ask if you can capture it on camera.

The gold standard is the **client who is happy to provide a phone or email introduction and then take a call for you.**

This is the best social proof you can have.

Nothing better than starting the conversation with someone who has been referred to you and having a lot in common by virtue of the fact that you both know a third party who brought you together. In addition, by being able with confidence to sit in front of your buyer and quote a number of examples of happy clients and then offering up a name and number for the buyer to call exudes authority in your solution.

It's not now you talking about how wonderful you are, it's your customer.

Most Won't Even Make the Call!

The strange thing about this process I have found is that on less than 25 percent of occasions does the prospective customer actually make the call to the advocate for your solution. It's the gesture made to the prospect that moves the buyer into action.

On the rare occasion that they do in fact actually make the call to the raving fan, I have found that you rarely don't then get the business. Consider it testing the water - once they make the call, it's all done.

The only thing of which to be cognisant is the communication you have set up in advance with the raving fan. To make this 100 percent effective, you need to spend the time having a conversation with the raving fan that they are going to have on your behalf.

Make it Easy for Them to Recommend You!

The secret is to make it easy for them. The most common question is, of course, 'What do you want me to say?' It's fine for them to say that they are happy to do it for you, but you need to now point them in the right direction. If my branding is "the trusted advisor in sales," I want the raving fan to say exactly that.

'You know, Brad has been a great sounding board to our sales manager and national sales team—he really has been their trusted advisor.' This soundbite is something I must brief the raving fan so it is congruent with your message to prospective customers. Prepare in advance—you want new clients to have a successful experience. The more precise you can make any third-party social proof appear to a prospective buyer, the more impact and the better chance of conversion.

For example, I see testimonials on websites or sales letters that simply say: "I have used …….. services over the last five years in business and would say their impact in my business has been a 54 percent increase in sales compounding year on year. If you are not using …….. services in your business right now, you are crazy."

Wonderful testimonial as it is, it then finishes with "Mr T, from Melbourne." Not a lot of value to the person reading it. It just falls flat.

How much credibility do you expect to create when you are not able to even put the person's name down on the quote? Pretty easy to make stuff up. Mr. S, Mr. A, these don't sound like real people to me!

Third-party social proof is almost like having an extra salesperson selling your message, selling your solution, and selling you personally. Done well, it's one of the most powerful pieces of theatre shared in this book.

Given that the Trusted Advisor Selling method is a good deal about getting referrals and trusted introductions, the ability to engage third-party help is critical to your success.

If this is something you are not good at, you are not alone.

I think in our culture we don't want to appear too pushy or slick in sales. Perhaps those who have sold before us with the subtle or not-so-subtle technique of manipulation have made buyers more wary and sellers more gun shy.

The asking for social proof from raving fans in itself is something that I have found great clients are really happy to do, they want to help.

It's really all in the language and approach we have spoken about before that will get results for you, and we just need to get past the reluctance. Think about how much money you are potentially leaving on the table by not taking action.

So start a list now of those clients who are really close raving fans—we all have them, we just need to identify them. Reach out to them and ask for a testimonial, perhaps create a reason as I have in the past.

A new website, a new promotion, a presentation to a new client.

Once you get that nailed down, go back to them in a stepped approach and gain their permission to take a call in the future from a prospect or two whom you are currently courting.

This will provide you with a high level of confidence from now on to go to market and as you uncover new opportunities. They may never actually get a call, but wow, now you are bullet proof.

As time goes on and the relationship is getting deeper and deeper with your raving fan, engage in the spirit of collaboration (another time to explain), where you now look for reciprocal arrangements and **cross refer to each other.**

Great Theatre of the Sale Tip:

Go to your customers now and ask them for a testimonial and create an excuse. Create a deeper conversation with someone who you have worked with for many years and ask them if it is okay for you to refer people you are talking to at the moment to them who would like to hear from a customer. Start the process, you will be amazed how easy it is.

The Assumptive Re-Confirmation

Is it just me or have your noticed that there are levels of confirmed appointments?

Whatever happened to those days when you would leave a meeting and you both opened up your diary and made the next appointment date in advance?

Recently, I had a client ask if I had sent them a calendar invite to the meeting direct to their diary when I phoned to re-confirm we were meeting that week. Apparently, if you don't send one these days, your meeting is never actually confirmed, even though you had agreement verbally on the time and the day. I understand that there is a similar rule in dating: if it's not re-confirmed or an invite accepted, it's not on?

I guess I am in a time warp. I was taught when you had agreement through a confirmed email and follow up phone call, we had both committed to it.

Not today. The etiquette of a promise or a handshake has been replaced with an invite. That's because we are all "so busy".

Here is the kicker: even when you have set up a meeting through the calendar and it is accepted by the buyer, it doesn't actually mean it's going ahead.

I had a customer just recently who rejected the meeting on the morning of a 10 a.m. meeting by the stroke of a few keys only 45 minutes before the meeting as something had suddenly come up! No phone call, no email, just a decline to the meeting invite which they had previously accepted. It was only when I phoned them to ask if it was an error (as I was already in traffic to the meeting) that the reply was simply, 'Oh yes, sorry, I have a meeting I have to now go to.'

The world has gone mad.

So… our objective in sales is still the same. It is to try and pour cement over the appointment and not let the buyer off the hook in a less loyal and ruder marketplace. My strategy has always been to remind the buyer of the upcoming meeting; the medium may have changed but the rules still apply. To gain leverage on the meeting and to ensure that they don't change their mind, it's our role as a proactive salesperson to let them know of what I have prepared in advance so they don't even consider cancelling the meeting.

On an email and on the phone, I may say:

'I am looking forward to our meeting, I have been doing a fair bit of work on (................), and I have some options to discuss and brainstorm.'

Pour the cement.

When you consider the investment in time and dollars to have that meeting at your client's premises and the cost of them not showing, changing their mind, or forgetting the meeting, it's not really smart to let the buyer off the hook by being sloppy and not nailing it down.

When your buyer recognises that you have invested some time and are not just showing up for a chat, the game changes. You could add a little more cement by sending them something to look at.

Again, it's all aimed to up the importance of the meeting. If you are bringing along a support team member to the meeting, mention it and the fact that the diaries all align.

More cement.

The assumptive re-confirmation won't work every time as not everyone plays ball with the correct business etiquette, but I work on making the meeting as fool proof as possible—I work on the percentages.

I want to make sure that not only have I got the best chance of them being there and not forgetting the meeting, I also want to make sure I don't have great slabs of time taken out of my diary as unproductive due to travelling distances, etc.

The theatre doesn't take long to set up—a short email, a text, and/or a phone call to make sure everything is in place.

Be proactive, jump on the front foot and re-confirm them.

We can't assume that any meeting will go ahead these days, but what we can do is create a process so we can ensure we are at the top of the tree when having our meetings confirmed.

When you consider the countless hours wasted in sales running around and no result being achieved through busy work, change the game.

Great Theatre of the Sale Tip:

Keep appointment times and re-confirm them. It's a show of professionalism and that your time and theirs is important. I often find the simple ideas are the ones that are overlooked in sales, and I can't remember the last time a salesperson or service provider who actually went to the trouble of doing this and risking the fact that I may not have been there.

Story Boarding

Ever found yourself making a pitch to a management team or board and had to take centre stage to present your ideas?

It can be nerve-racking for new players—you are right out there on show and you'd better catch their attention!

Flipcharts, whiteboard, and PowerPoint all at play with transitions of your points and perhaps creating a show in tandem with a fellow team member.

When I was a trainer with Dale Carnegie training in their *How to Win Friends and Influence People* program in the 90s, I saw first-hand the lather people can get themselves into before speaking to a group. Reminds me of that old saying, the number one fear in life is public speaking.

People would rather die than speak in public! So apart from practicing over and over again, how do we make sure that our presentation has real power and maximum theatre?

I have a technique that I have shown salespeople to use over the years in my Winning the Pitch workshops.

It has been to story board your presentation and to plan ahead for the impact you are aiming to make.

You know how we talked earlier about the being the director of your own sales call?

Story boarding is a technique that TV production companies have used for years to plan how the episode on TV would play out. They were used widely by the creative team for commercials or comic sketches to conceptually see what the finished product might look like before going into final planning and shooting.

Pitching for business is like planning a performance for an audience or a commercial—it is the texture of the sales call or presentation.

So how does the story board idea work? In days gone by on TV, it involved a series of actual boards being used with each scene being played out on a separate board and then you can see how it all flows.

I am sure today there is some funky software that can do it for you, but I am old school and love to have the tactile nature of paper and board in front of me.

My opinion has always been that it is the end result I am looking for, the outcome.

So here is my method. Take a bunch of sticky notes of different colours or the traditional 4x6 cards with different colours. Any newsagent will sell them.

Divide the cards into piles that represent different elements of theatre in the presentation to keep the audience engaged.

For example:

- Green cards – stories
- Red cards – quotes or evidence
- Yellow cards – PowerPoint
- Blue cards – questions
- Pink cards - use of flipchart/whiteboard
- White cards - handouts/collateral

Now brainstorm all your ideas for the presentation and get them down, start to mind map, and arrange your ideas.

Think about where you think a bit of content will work, the PowerPoint, etc. How about an opportunity to ask questions… where would that make sense?

Keep exploring what a great presentation would look like, how would you get feedback or get them to discuss a concept? As you arrange the ideas, pop them on the appropriate cards or coloured sticky notes and then sort them into an order that you think might work for the presentation.

Look at the texture of the presentation now… is it heavy in certain places? Or does it need something to make it come to life? Arrange the flow onto a white board or wall and see if it makes sense. Most likely you will be too heavy on information, perhaps too much PowerPoint? Each year I make presentations to CEO groups that might last for one hour with approximately 12 – 15 CEOS sitting around a board table, imparting ideas for them to consider for use in their own companies.

When I started out making these presentations I would fill them with content from my PowerPoint to make me look smart. The only problem was that even though the content was solid and it show me as an authority on the subject, you can lose your audience.

These people were busy and there was always a lot going on back at the office. To get them to attend these meetings each month for a half day at a time was hard for the organisers.

I had to change the texture of the presentation and make sure at any point I didn't talk for more than about 7–10 minutes and then get feedback, ask a question here and there, and see whether the topic I was presenting was resonating with them. This chunking of the presentation really helped with gaining a number of leads and opportunities for more work.

Is the "one to many" something you should be exploring? Is it something that you need to get better at? Story boarding will help to arrange your ideas.

Great Theatre of the Sale Tip:

Storyboarding gives you a sneak look at how the performance will flow; it alerts you to what is missing or what needs to change. Next time you have a more formal presentation, map it out first with the outcome and how your presentation will deliver on that outcome. Seeing it all in front of you allows you to determine whether you are on the right track to deliver the magic of great theatre.

Good, Better, Best

Having presented your ideas convincingly, there comes a point when you have to drive agreement. Some people feel awkward about asking, but if you've defined the situation before arriving, followed by a well-crafted performance, the agreement is the only logical conclusion.

It is now time to be the solution-recommender.

If you go online, you'll find a long list of types of closes. There's the Assumptive Close (assuming the deal has been made), the Now or Never Close (it won't be there later), the Objection Close ("Is there any reason why you wouldn't buy?"), the Summary Close (which is what it sounds like), and a useful list of maybe 40 different ways of wrapping up a sale.

In my workshops, I teach 12 that I am fond of. They're all good when appropriate, but here's one that's worked well for me: I like to confirm the sale with "good, better, best."

My father always taught me that when people have three alternatives, they invariably will pick one. They have the choice of yeses, whereas when people are confronted with a yes/no option, it's too easy for them to choose "NO." Buyers switch off when it's complicated. Early in my sales career, my dad said to me, 'Brad, a confused mind does not buy. So, it's a three-option close, not four, not five… just three.'

That's why he taught me the three-step process of good, better, and best. By giving the buyer three ways to say yes, there is an inference in the conversation that they will indeed go ahead with one of the options. It's just a matter of which one! That's a considerable mind shift to start with.

Two-thirds of this is theatre. I use two options to steer people in the direction of where I want them to go. Going into the conversation, I have planned out the three options with the middle option always looking the most attractive to the buyer.

1. **"Good"** is the first alternative. It's the most economical, it's the plain and sensible one. It's also the cheapest.

2. **"Better"** is next, priced about 20 percent more than good.
3. **"Best"** is top of the range and can be up to 50 percent more.

If you provide good, better, and best, on average about two-thirds of the time, they will take the "better" option because "good" feels too cheap and maybe it doesn't give them all the bells and whistles they want.

"Best" might be above their budget constraints. But still offer it. My father would say, "You might get a surprise! You might be smoking cigars!" In other words, sometimes you'll fall off your chair because the person has agreed to buy something you didn't think they'd buy. In fact, I can remember many sales calls where the buyer not only bought the "best" option, but if I had another "best plus" up my sleeve that was beyond the "yes" (for example, a "fantastic" or "awesome" option), they would have bought that as well.

It challenges you to create one right there in front of them when you know and can see they are in buying mode and nothing is going to stop them!

It's important to realise that we make big assumptions about what budget people have and what they can afford. You may just get a big surprise.

An example of this was the newsletter publisher, Huntley Publishing, who sold by direct mail. They offered a one-year subscription price, two years, and five. Hardly anyone ever ticked the five-year option, but Huntley always put it on the client response card as an option because—joy of joys!—every now and then, someone would actually tick it! That's money for jam!

The thinking behind the "good, better, best" strategy is that you are really crafting your offering of solutions to make it compelling for them to take the middle option. It represents a compromise from the entry level to the really premium option. People don't want to appear like cheapskates, countered by not wanting to break the budget.

This is one of the overlooked opportunities for salespeople to make substantially more margin in a sale and this is really important when you consider that more and more salespeople are not being paid on gross margin rather than gross sales dollars.

Selling in Unique Packages

The magic in creating three options is your ability to craft unique packages. It's like the bookkeeper who says that you cannot charge more than $55 per hour (which I was told a little while ago by a client) for bookkeeping services. Not true. 'Why are you charging by the hour, anyway?' I responded.

When I chose my last bookkeeper, I was only concerned with one thing: what is the monthly investment I need to allow for in my budget for your services? Let's agree on say $500 per month. I now have no concern about how long or short you spend on my books. As long as I have my books up to date and everything is balancing and paid on time, etc., what do I care?

We get way too obsessed with hourly rates, the worst way to sell your services. It's also the least entrepreneurial as it gives you no incentive to find a better and quicker way to complete a task. It's counterproductive to your income. So now think of your offers in packages and make them unique. Give them unique names as well to create a little proprietary language.

Once you have the packages, price them so that the middle one looks really attractive, perhaps it has something you know all clients want. Now the important bit: price it only 20 percent max above the good level. Twenty percent seems to be a palatable increase in premium from the good level in my experience.

People can usually afford it.

The other outcome the good, better, and best strategy can create is the need for a hybrid option, which may be a combination of these options that you might not have thought of. Leave your mind open to it and be flexible while talking through the options with the customer as it may be one of the new options you can now offer up to all your customers!

So you now craft the new hybrid package, well, the process may start again. No reason why the new hybrid package can't have a couple of add-ons which then make it into a new good, better, and best. By framing up the good, better, best strategy with something like, 'There are three recommendations for you to consider in moving forward,' then explaining them, you are now being the trusted advisor. Then simply letting them know that option two sounds like the best way forward based on what they just explained to you makes perfect sense to them.

Great Theatre of the Sale Tip:

Presenting three options really gives you every chance of making the sale, the theatre of it is in the delivery and the planning of the three options. List all the things that could be in your deluxe option and then start to take things away as you determine the good and better options. Remember the assumption here that they will go ahead with one of the three.

The "Agreement in Principle"

It's time to play one more role: The Influencer.

Not the manipulative closer—a person who is genuinely thinking of the best way forward for the customer, that's the trusted advisor mind-set. The first part of the agreement in principle is all about "testing the water." It means sticking your toe in the pool. Test your prospect's interest temperature.

Find out where s/he sits on the buying continuum. You may even be there right now—your buyer might already come up with a favourable response!

As the trusted advisor, we want what is in our solution to be a good match with the customer's needs and wants.

Testing the water allows us to know what needs to be present in the solution, in other words, to honour the rule that we are in the results business and not the proposals business.

The "agreement in principle" is all about taking the meeting dance of all possibilities and brings the conversation into a funnel where you sort out the ideas and map a way forward.

The truth is that some sales can't be made there and then on the spot. In large scale business-to-business decisions, there may be multiple influencers that need to be involved and budgets to work within. Complexity of the solution will probably involve multiple departments in the co-ordination of the total solution.

Our goal is to walk out of the meeting with an "agreement in principle" of the budget range, what it will contain, the deliverables, and timing. It's not a formal commitment, no signed contract at this point, just a meeting of the minds conceptually to move forward to the next stage.

Perhaps it's something as simple as re-summarising the next action steps, what you will go away and work on. But… it's a little more than that:

You are looking for a commitment in principle in return for doing the work.

So how do we do deliver this approach?

Here are three examples of how we can move a buyer into agreement of the solution and on the next steps:

You might say to the buyer,

'In an ideal world, which option sounds right to you?'

In other words, I'm not going to hold the buyer to it but, after considering all options, where are we heading? Some buyers will say, 'I like that option, but I've got champagne taste with a beer budget.' And that's okay. Using the words **'I recommend…'** is another way of getting agreement in principle from your buyer.

Now you are a problem-solver, offering a solution that points to the close. It's conceptual because your recommendation isn't absolute. It's based on what they've told you.

Perhaps we get agreement from the buyer to move ahead with a deeper commitment? Something like, **'Let's say we can get that first order through to you by Friday, could we then have a conversation about the larger contract?'**

In other words, if we can prove ourselves, could we have a bigger conversation? This book began with the definition of the situation.

I am now asking for a redefinition: 'If everything goes well, can we do this too?'

How about … **'If we can provide a competitive bid, would we be a candidate for your business?'**

There is something I have always liked about this approach. You are not asking for a commitment to be the only choice, but you are asking to be considered. I find this particularly useful when you are talking with someone who is genuinely happy with their current supplier and you are trying to shake the buyer awake.

"Agreement in principle" short cuts the conversation by pre-qualifying the prospect into a deeper conversation.

It says to the buyer, 'I need to know if you are really serious about doing business together or we just wasting each other's time.'

There are times when we can be more assertive with this approach, in terms of creating and moving the "agreement in principle" to trial close in old language.

You might say something like this:

1. **'If I can get approval, are we okay to do the paperwork?'**
2. **'By the sounds of things, we're a good fit. Can we move forward with the agreement?'**
3. **'If you were to proceed at this point, which option do you like?'**
4. **'I'm not saying I can, but if I could…?'**

These questions are designed to test the water and find out how hot or cold your prospect is. You can use them word for word or you can tweak them to suit your approach. Make it your own—add and subtract words, adapt everything until it comes across naturally.

The rubber has now hit the road in the performance, when the customer experience now has to move forward with a commitment or we have wasted our time. It starts with belief in the part one is playing (salesperson or buyer) and climaxes with letting buyers see their future possibilities.

The trusted advisor knows that it saves a whole lot of time if you can get the buyer to agree in principle to what you are recommending and not having to go back and forth in future sales calls and written communications.

So many sales are lost in the back and forward, there is too much time to change your mind as the buyer.

Assertive buyers might also just get bored or impatient with the elongated process and think to themselves, 'Do they not want my business?'

We are in the results business and not in the proposals business, and so this means we need to be bold at times.

When we hang on tightly to lukewarm opportunities, they take the place of other possibilities of new business from people who really want to do business with us. When sales people hang on tight, I often think they haven't created enough in the pipeline, so they are holding on at all costs to all opportunities.

Great Theatre of the Sale Tip:

Ask about it point blank: 'What would you like to see in the future?' Be bold, ask the question. It's part of the theatre we are performing. In most cases, your buyer will respect the fact that you are trying to create a meeting of the minds between the two of you which, in the long term, saves you both wasting your time.

SO BRING YOUR THEATRE TO LIFE!

Great theatre is inside of each of us.

It elevates the salesperson into a performer, and when you master some of these ideas covered in this book, you become the Trusted Advisor.

In an age of commoditisation and speed, where business moves fast and decisions can be based on a spreadsheet after putting in all the variables of price from each vendor, this book has aimed to push back against commoditisation and to help the salesperson differentiate.

I have never been someone who has tried to be the cheapest and I don't want to get into a price war as there is always someone out there prepared to do it cheaper and cheaper.

Perhaps you have found yourself there over and over again and you were looking for a proactive way of being in a category of one—maybe there is a technique in Part B where you can try a new approach and get the results immediately.

The parallels of theatre and selling are argued in Part A, and I hope that I have provided clarity around the characters, the script, the set, the props, the director, and choreographing of the performance with that of a sales experience that can be created on a sales call.

Be the director of your sales call—start to craft what you would like to see as the fabric and texture of that interaction with your client and prospect. I guarantee it will make you more memorable and, in my experience, that adds up to more sales.

There is no limit to theatre, it only comes down to your imagination and your courage to try things. Good luck.

Additional resources and tools to help you convert more sales

Here's how to experience more of the Brad Tonini Trusted Advisor Selling Method:-

Website - www.bradtonini.com

The Monday Morning Mojo - our weekly video program

Weekly sales program – NewSelling

Join our LinkedIn Group – The Trusted Sales Advisor

Brad's Trusted Advisor Selling Institute runs:-

A monthly "Friday School of Sales" breakfast

A number of half and full day programs in the Trusted Advisor Selling Method

Virtual and face to face sales training for your sales team

The Sales Leaders Roundtable – an intensive groups of sales managers and business owners mastermind program

www.ingramcontent.com/pod-product-compliance
Ingram Content Group UK Ltd.
Pitfield, Milton Keynes, MK11 3LW, UK
UKHW020143250726
13967UKWH00002B/845

9 780648 911203